A GIRL NAMED MISHKA

A GIRL NAMED MISHKA

CLARENCE CARTER

CHAPTER ONE

Frigid wind whistled around Ivana Ressala's ears. With the baby wrapped tightly in a pink blanket, plumes of vapor wisped from her lips. She'd been crying for nearly two hours. Her body trembled. Her tiny heart pounded against Ivana's chest. Ivana's exhausted tears froze to her face. The long country road led to the woods she played in as a child. Glistening snow covered the forest floor as she trudged deeper into its shade. Ghostly bare trees crackled. Mishka's cries echoed through the woods.

Never in her life had she run this far, or this fast. *Not fast enough.* With every step, snow plunged in her boots.

Rocking her baby, Ivana whispered, "Everything's going to be alright."

Hollow footprints trailed in thick snow. Ivana pressed Mishka's tiny body tight to her chest. Parenthood hadn't been anything like she expected. She never imagined doing it alone. Heroin had played its role, too.

The addiction decimated her life, fast. Regret and fear swarmed her head like hornets. Nothing could have prepared her for this. Jagged gasps heaved in and out of her lungs, sharp like pins. Her mind retreated to a better place.

A lifetime ago, in the same woods, she'd played with her brother Anton. They'd chase each other around the biggest tree. They'd played tag for hours or go on adventures together.

The cold wind whipped her face raw. Crying and running had depleted her. Collapse wasn't only possible but inevitable.

A little further.

Every muscle screamed for mercy. Her legs had never felt heavier. Not even when she'd carried Mishka in her womb did her back ache with such ferocity.

The tree, a staple of her childhood, loomed in the distance. Ivana forced herself to carry on, growing closer. Behind her came a rustling that ran her blood cold. Knowing time had ran out, she began to pray.

Oh God, please don't let them kill my baby.

Two hours hadn't been enough of a head start. The thugs found her anyway. Her scatterbrained plan of escape didn't work and now she had to suffer the consequences. Flashlight beams danced in her periphery. They were close.

Quivering lips kissed Mishka's rosy cheek. "I'm going to lead them away. When the sun comes up, scream as loud as you can. Someone will find you."

Ivana's words fell on deaf ears. Mishka couldn't understand because she was only an infant. Ivana couldn't believe that. Wouldn't believe that.

If there'd been more time, things would have gone differently. She could have found a home for Mishka. A loving family who would raise her right. She deserved that.

Over her shoulder, Ivana searched for the bundle lying against the tree. Her heart broke. There were a million things she wanted to say, but no time to say them. She'd daydreamed about watching her grow up. She just couldn't turn it around.

A distant bark shredded the silence. Ivana sprinted. She hadn't anticipated dogs. Immense pain riddled her neck from looking over her shoulder for two hours. Intentionally she made noise, drawing them away from her baby. Her forbidden baby.

Flashlight beams raced through the trees. Voices bounced off the trunks. Branches clawed and scraped as she dashed through them like a madwoman. They gained on her.

Unable to run any longer, Ivana collapsed. The babies wail resonated through the snow-covered trees. She hadn't lured them far enough. The last thing she heard were the desperate shrieks of her baby girl before they killed her.

CHAPTER TWO

Kansas City, Missouri.

The bell rang through the halls of St. Seraphim. The school had a reputation for being the school for troubled kids or those who fell between the cracks. Lester Klass belonged there more than any of them. He had a fascination with the morbid. Things other kids shuddered at Lester found hilarious. This didn't make him popular with the other children, or the teachers. Although they'd never say it aloud, some of them feared him.

From an early age, Lester's mother knew he was trouble. A couple of times he'd been caught peeking under the stalls in the girls' room. He'd also found a dead cat on the side of the road and poked its insides with a stick.

When it came to punishment, Lester seemed rather blasé.

At her wits end, Virginia Klass pulled the boy from public school and moved him to St. Seraphim. No book would help, no therapist could reach him. Virginia hoped the Lord would intervene, but he hadn't.

As he walked the halls, his sneakers scuffed the tile floor. He didn't look up from the checkered pattern. Rarely did he make eye contact with anyone.

Lester lacked sympathy, empathy, or any emotion a normal child would display. He especially lacked fear. He'd been beaten senseless by bullies but continued to instigate them. Some teachers called him masochistic. Lester's mouth was one of his best weapons, far superior to his fists. He had a way with words, considerably witty for his age.

As if his disposition wasn't enough, he also had attributes other kids found hysterical. Red hair, freckles, and the pale skin of an Irishman like his father. He was also small for his age.

The classroom filled with eager children, excited for summer vacation. A lot of them mentioned video games and trips afar. Lester couldn't relate. He hadn't been anywhere. Even when they spoke of the newest videogames, he couldn't relate to that either. He'd lost that privilege long ago.

A girl by the name of Laura Hampton sat in front of him. A pretty little spitfire with hair that smelled of green apple. The entire school knew of Lester's crush on her. Everyone except her, which Lester thanked God for routinely. As far as he could tell, she knew nothing of the love letters he'd written but long ago discarded.

As the class progressed, Lester stared at her and fantasized, paying less and less attention to the teacher.

Ms. Goldstein stood at the front of the class, lecturing about literature. Books had never been much of Lester's interest unless they were obscene. He read *Dracula* to its completion and considered the possibility of vampires. To a child of only ten, it all seemed plausible. He struggled with the big words but extracted all the graphic scenes. He particularly loved the gore and blood. On a few occasions, he tasted his own, especially after taking a beating.

The green apple shampoo. The pretty smile. Lester tried to imagine what it would be like to hold her hand, to be seen with her. All the thoughts that followed weren't as flattering as kissing her when the teachers weren't looking.

She wouldn't be seen with me.

The bell rang, releasing him to the wild. Walking through the halls, he kept a keen eye on the other students. Sometimes he felt like an alien because he didn't fit in. Their interactions always baffled him.

Outside by the bus pickup, people hugged and talked amongst themselves. That certainly hadn't been his experience. When encountering other children, he'd usually been met with ridicule and fists. In public school, they'd even given him a nickname "Shark Eyes" which confused and intrigued him. Hours of staring into the mirror didn't clarify it.

Cars whizzed by as he meandered home, one of the few freedoms he had left. Videogames and outside activities had been taken. He'd also been kicked off the bus. Lester suspected his mother would have preferred to drive him, that way she could keep an eye on him. Her job wouldn't allow that.

Down the block from the school was a fenced yard and a dog named Hercules. A drooly Cane Corso with eyes like coal. Mr. Forest, the owner of said dog, much like everyone in his life, wasn't a fan of Lester. Several times he'd ran his hands through the links and even growled at Hercules, taunting him. Mr. Forest didn't like this behavior and usually hollered at him from the shade of his porch.

Again, the chain links rattled under his fingertips. He didn't look up to meet the old man's gaze, only listened for the growl. Through his periphery he kept an eye on the man and his mongrel.

It hopped off the porch, ran twenty feet or so and growled. Its hackles stood ridged. Its sharp bark penetrated his ears, making him wince.

You're going to pay for trying to scare me.

"Easy, boy," Mr. Forest said. Hercules retreated, climbing the rickety steps and laying at his feet. Gangly fingers ran across the dogs back, smoothing its fur.

I'm not afraid of you.

With no rhyme or reason, a storm brewed inside Lester. He came from a loving family, both parents present. He didn't have a father who drank excessively, or a mother who beat him.

The guidance counselor once wrote, "*Mr. Klass is evil for the sake of evil.*" In the same notes, she also recommended drugs, many of them, and high doses. Sedatives.

The drugs left him tired and somehow incomplete. A void he couldn't express in words. Like he'd lost something but couldn't remember what or where. At times, he considered he'd lost a part of himself.

Sluggish, Lester walked through the front door, feet dragged with every step. He hadn't gotten the chance to torment Hercules, not with that old fuck watching. One day, Lester swore he'd make that dog pay. One day it would learn.

Deep in the chasm of his imagination, Lester saw the dog as a three headed dragon. He saw himself as the knight.

Virginia sat up from her position on the couch, ignoring *Sex and the City*. "Les, dear, are you okay?"

Such questions always perplexed Lester, who wasn't sure he'd ever felt *okay*. "I don't know," he said with a shrug. The bag clashed on the floor. A succession of footsteps resonated as he climbed the stairs. Pictures of himself at T-ball stared back at him.

She called after him. "Hold up, mister."

The footsteps stopped. Those brown eyes peered over the railing, locks of red hair strewn across his face. "Yes?"

Sarah Jessica Parker rambled on the screen as Virginia got a better look. "Your teacher called today. She said you had a great day."

Disinterested, Lester continued up the stairs, closing the bedroom door behind him. Alone. He'd always enjoyed being alone, which had been concerning to his mother.

He couldn't tell her why it had been a good day. The last thing he wanted to do was explain his good behavior was because of a girl. If he wanted to hold her hand, he'd have to make a lot of changes. A part of him didn't think he'd ever get there because he struggled resisting his urges.

Not long after, his mother called him down for dinner as she put on the finishing touches.

Liver and onion permeated the kitchen as Virginia worked diligently. A steak sizzled on the pan for Lester's father, who hated liver.

Sitting idly by, waiting for their meal, Lester stared off into space. Something he did often. Memories of a videogame long taken came and went. Thoughts of the girl. And thoughts of Hercules.

Virginia paused for a second, staring at the block. "One of the knives is missing," she mused. "Your father must have forgotten it in his office or something." She shook her head.

Forks and knives scraped the plates. They stared at him, which always made Lester uncomfortable. Part of him wanted to lash out, scream at them to mind their own damn business, but he didn't.

With a bloody hunk of meat on his fork, Steve asked, "How's school?"

Lester shrugged.

Serving herself another scoop of mashed potatoes, Virginia asked, "What are you learning right now?"

Lester shrugged, stabbing the onions with his fork. He didn't look up. Rarely did he look up from his plate. If they were going to get something out of him, they'd have to surgically remove it. The meal concluded without much more revelations about his day.

School went without a hitch. He tried to maintain that good boy image, but it all bottled up. Laura, if she knew he existed at all, made no mention of his two good days. This infuriated him. That anger and resentment weighed heavily. He resisted his urges once again, containing the beast for a little longer.

CHAPTER THREE

Serpukhov, Russia.

With the sun barely cresting the horizon, an older couple walked their Malamute puppy through the snow. Thick, wet flakes fell from the sky. They laughed, bundled in their warmest clothes. She had an arm wrapped around his.

He loved how the snow glistened in the trees beyond the road. The snow would stop later in the day and they would be able to see all of its glory.

Wind whipped her gray hair. "It's really coming down."

With a nod, he said, "Yeah, supposed to be freezing all night."

Valeria pulled him closer.

Albert wiped flakes off his glasses as the dog tugged the leash. The puppy sniffed the ground, barked joyously, and snipped at the air. They stared at him, hoping he would quit playing and hurry up. They both agreed getting a dog was a great idea. Aside from walking him in the cold, he'd been the greatest companion. It enhanced their golden years.

A single car whizzed by, too fast for a road as slick as theirs. After it turned out of sight, the dogs ears perked up. Albert looked curiously at the dog, imagining a bird had fluttered from the trees or something.

Valeria turned to the woods. "Did you hear that?"

Tugging at the leash, reeling the dog in, he shook his head. "It's just the wind."

The dogs ears twitched again. "It's just the wind, huh?" She pointed at the dog, who'd stepped closer to the woods and the noise beyond. A long pause fell between them before she asked, "Is that a baby crying?"

An image of a woman pushing a stroller crossed his mind. Albert chuckled. "A baby, out here? That's absurd."

It happened again.

His face turned to stone. The leash clattered on the ground. Before he knew what he was doing, he'd bound into the snow. His heart thrummed like it hadn't in years. Unmistakable shrieks filled the air.

As he got closer, they got louder. Frantically looking left and right, he proceeded through the bare trees. *Keep crying,* he thought. *Just a little longer.* The wind and rustling branches made it difficult to follow the noise.

Deeper and deeper he tracked into the woods. Gradually the cries got louder. The dog trailed beside him, hopping through thick powder.

Lying at the base of a tree he caught sight of a pink blanket half buried. The puppy lapped at the little, wailing bundle. Angry feet kicked beneath the cloth and for a second, he couldn't believe his eyes. Never in all his years had he seen someone discard a baby in such a way.

In disbelief, Albert knelt down and touched it with a trembling hand. Carefully, he unzipped his jacket and tucked the baby under the wing of his coat, hoping his body heat would warm it. The wails continued, loud, obnoxious sobs. Each cry ear-piercing and brutal.

The tracks had been covered by a fresh layer of snow. If there'd been a parent, they were long gone, and they weren't coming back.

Snow crunched under his boots as he navigated toward the road.

Gently he rocked and shushed her as he walked. The dog trailed a couple of steps behind. Against his body, she trembled and kicked.

He rubbed the infants back, thinking about how deathly sick she could get. Cold wind shot daggers at his face, and he wondered just how long she'd been out there. No matter what he tried, she wouldn't stop crying.

Albert emerged from the woods with the bundle under his coat. She squirmed and protested. Stepping onto the road, he shushed her again.

Shock riddled Valeria's face. "Is it?"

Solemnly, he nodded.

They trekked the quarter-mile home. Valeria took the dog in her arms so they could move quicker. The baby howled as they went. Humming didn't work, nor rocking. He imagined she wouldn't stop crying for a long time, not even when she'd gotten dry.

The fire roared. Albert and Valeria got to work with a youthful quickness. First, he pulled the wet clothes off the baby, discarding the diaper. Luckily, he didn't see any signs of frostbite. Aside from a mean diaper rash, she looked fine. In the flickering firelight he noticed an embroidery on the pink blanket. "Mishka."

Mishka is a boy's name, he thought. But he'd definitely undressed a girl. Towels and clean linens came in a hurry. Valeria wrapped her up tight, running the dry towel across her body with a soft, soothing touch.

They didn't have baby clothes, so they made do.

Pointing to the blanket, Albert whispered, "Her name is Mishka."

Amused, Valeria snorted before heading for the kitchen.

Albert stoked the fire, hoping to get the house warm enough to settle her.

The whir of a blender rang through the house as Valeria made baby food. They'd had children once upon a time and knew what to do. Their children were long since grown and had kids of their own, much older than Mishka.

Kneeling down with a bowl of food, Valeria whispered, "Miracle baby."

After an hours' worth of work, she stopped crying. They'd successfully fed her and gotten her wrapped up in warm, clean wraps. They planned on getting her baby clothes in the morning.

Stoking his pipe, Albert whispered, "You know we can't keep her." Smoke rose over his head.

Briefly, he thought he saw that sparkle in her eye die. They both knew it wouldn't work. Their youth was behind them, and babies were too much work. Even a puppy had proven to be a handful.

Although he didn't drink much, Albert fetched some liquor to calm his nerves. Vodka poured over crackling ice. Smoke rolled from the bowl of his pipe as he stared into the fire, contemplating what kind of a monster would leave a baby to die.

Long after Valeria went to bed, Albert stared into the fire. Mishka lie on her back, fast asleep. He'd have to make an appointment to get her checked out. Luckily the frostbite hadn't started on her extremities.

We got there just in time.

Throughout the night, Albert didn't leave her side. He slept on the couch with her on the floor beside him. As expected, he didn't sleep much.

CHAPTER FOUR

Kansas City, Missouri.

"That boy did this!" *With a quivering hand, Mr. Forest pointed at Lester. "He hurt my baby. My poor Hercules." The look on his mother's face told him everything he needed to know. What he'd done was unforgivable.*

In the middle of the night, Lester ran away. He only packed a few things. He couldn't imagine staying there, having to look his mother in the eye when she wore that disappointed, brokenhearted look.

Grumbling to himself, Lester said, "I fuckin' hate that place. Good riddance."

Lester's stomach ached with waves of hunger. Dizziness swept over him. He hadn't eaten lunch at school. Instead, he'd given it to Laura. She thanked him, which started as a kind gesture. He overstayed his welcome at her table, and her friends got angry. He didn't take kindly to their hostility and had another outburst. He got into an argument with the other children and lashed out at Cory Hill.

It wasn't until after Lester called Cory's mother a whore that he pondered its meaning. It was one of those words often thrown together with other inappropriate words without context. Angry, Lester paced the hall, trying to calm himself.

Then, he decided to take everything out on Hercules, the same mutt that threatened him every time he walked by. The one who Lester was certain would eat him, given the chance. Several times throughout the walk Lester revisited this memory.

The sun cast pink streaks into the sky. His stomach rumbled with every step. Thinking ahead had never been his strong suit and he hadn't prepared to run away. The salty scent of fries and burgers lingered on the air.

A luminescent sign hung overhead, advertising the local burger joint. If not for his lack of funds, Lester would have walked right up to the counter.

A voice came from behind the restaurant. "Psst, hey, Lester. Come over here."

Without seeing the face behind the voice, Lester felt a bit hesitant. "What?"

"Come here, jerk," he said.

Hesitant, Lester walked into the alley where he saw David Coleman. The kid he'd been friends with at the beginning of the school year. Their friendship ended when Coleman had taken Lester's favorite toy car. He was a scrawny kid, short hair. He had a small head with big eyes. The two hadn't spoken for some time, and the grudge had dwindled.

Those sticky fingers had cost them their friendship. Lester had sworn his revenge but had forgotten. All of his energy had gone toward the dog.

Looking around at the alley he asked, "What do you want, David?"

For only twelve, David proved to be one hell of a thief. A frayed toothpick hung from his mouth. David leaned against the wall. Dirty, ripped jeans clung to his stick legs.

He flicked the toothpick into a heap of trash. "I figured we could help each other out."

Taking another look around, Lester asked, "How's that?"

A pack of smokes came from his shirt pocket. They looked like they'd been run over. He swatted one out and stuck it in his mouth. Lester couldn't help watching this charade with disgust.

A book of matches came from his dirty flannel. "See that group of girls?"

Leaning against the building, Lester stole a glance. He shrugged. "Yeah. So?"

A group of girls sat at the table throwing fries and giggling. They were older girls and pretty ones at that. Out of the group, Lester recognized one, not by name, only by face. Likely he'd seen her walking to the high school in the mornings.

The match struck, wafting sulfur about.

The first puff of smoke escaped his lips. "I need you to go over there and talk to them."

"Me?" Lester shrieked. "I can't do that." Overstaying his welcome at Laura's table reminded him of how well he did with others. The wound was still fresh, still painful.

Two fingers clutched the cigarette like he'd been doing it for years. "Yes, you can. Just for a minute."

Before he could protest, David pushed him out in the open. All of the girls looked. The sun hurt his eyes. A distant thought of pissing himself came as he stared at them, jaw flexing like a fish out of water.

One of the girls sneered. "Well, are you going to say something, or not, geek?" These girls were quite a bit older and more developed. They had boobs and shiny hair. One of them looked like she belonged on TV. "Speak, geek," the pretty girl hissed.

The others laughed.

"Ah, umm." Lester stammered. His face burned with embarrassment. Fear that he'd never find the words rushed over him. "Ah." They caught in his throat, and he would have given anything to push them out. Time slowed down as their gazes burned.

The mean girls asked, "Cat got your tongue?"

One of them threw a fry at him.

It smacked him right in the forehead.

Then a second.

Lester's temper warmed up. Blood rushed to his cheeks, and he was sure his face turned red. He tried to force something out, anything. He managed a croak, not quite a word. In his head, he screamed.

Say something.

More fries bounced off his chest, landing on the hot concrete below. One of them stuck her tongue out. They called him names. Loser. Dweeb. A couple he'd never heard before.

His grinding teeth brought forth a mean headache. The whimpering dog and the detached eyeball came to mind. The immense feeling of power. He wanted them to whimper, too. To feel his wrath.

The girls were busy laughing and didn't see it coming. Lester approached the leader, close enough to smell her perfume. A single kick. The plastic leg of her chair snapped, and she plummeted to the ground. Their laughs were replaced by gasps. With her sitting on the ground, they'd fallen silent. For a brief second Lester saw up her jean skirt. He didn't have time for such pleasantries.

Fear gleamed in her eyes, but that wasn't enough to satisfy his hunger for power. Standing over her, he wanted more. She didn't fear him like Hercules did.

A Styrofoam cup sat on the table in front of him. He grabbed it and flicked off the cover. Thick pink liquid poured out, sloshing over her head. Strawberry milkshake dribbled off her hair and down the front of her shirt. Tears had welled in her eyes.

Without looking back, Lester returned to the alley.

A few seconds passed before David came around the opposite corner. He had a purse clutched under his arm. "That's not what I had in mind."

A filthy hand shuffled through the belongings. Clearly irritated by the junk inside, David tipped it upside down. The contents spilled with a clatter. Mascara, tampons, compact mirror, and money. Two crumpled tens.

David handed one of them to Lester. "I think we should get out of here before they call the cops."

At this, Lester shrugged. "I think they're already looking for me."

Concern crossed David's face. "Thanks for the distraction."

Lester emerged from the alley after glancing around the corner. They were gone, but their trash remained. Clumps of milkshake still sat on the hot blacktop. Fries and burgers were left abandoned.

Casually, he walked inside, hoping they wouldn't be there. The people inside were clueless. They were caught up in their little worlds, absorbed by jobs, stocks and grown-up things. When he was certain nobody knew what he'd done, he approached the counter.

A teen girl with braces took his order. He bought burgers and fries and sat at the window, staring out at the damage he'd caused. A plastic chair with a broken leg and a milkshake baking in the sun. The remnants of food had attracted pigeons.

Lester basked in the hatred. He loved it, and it consumed him, leaving behind that coppery taste of anger. Placing fear in people gave him a rush. The thunderous beat of his heart made him feel alive, combatting that drowsy feeling from the medication.

Riding that high, Lester considered returning to Mr. Forests house and finishing the job. He wondered if he could instill fear in the old man, too. As the sun descended behind some buildings, the rage reduced to a simmer.

Lester hadn't gotten two blocks from the burger joint before his mother's car flew around the corner. One fender stood out. Primer white against red paint. The brakes screamed as it came to a stop. She hopped out and raced toward him. Her hair bounced as she ran. Her face had gone stoic. Lester wanted to run but couldn't.

Alright, bitch. This isn't the same Lester as before.

A vein in her neck bulged and her face had gone crimson. He'd never seen her that mad. "You get in that car, right now."

With conviction, Lester said, "No. You don't tell me what to do anymore." He paused, making unwavering eye contact. "I'm in charge now."

Bewilderment crossed her face before she snatched his earlobe and dragged him. In seconds, the paper tiger crumbled. Tears ran and he screamed in a tantrum. The warrior who'd fought off the beast nothing more than a memory.

She looked at him through the rearview. "What you did..." The anger started to slip. "To that poor dog." Tears streamed down her face. "I can't believe it."

CHAPTER FIVE

Serpukhov, Russia.

Outside the orphanages window, snow fell from the roof. With the phone pressed to her cheek, Olga nodded in disbelief. Her jaw hung loosely. "Uh, huh." Pause. "And you're absolutely certain of this?"

Her whole world had turned upside down in a matter of days. The DNA results had returned from the lab, and they matched their "miracle baby" to Victor Kerensky, one of the most feared men in Russia. Considering there hadn't been any news about his wife being pregnant, Olga figured Mishka wasn't a wanted or planned pregnancy.

Olga Sokolov begged the doctor not to inform him. She feared he would come looking for her. It didn't take much to figure out why she'd been left to die. He was a bad man, and she didn't want his thugs knocking on the door of the orphanage. Her yellowed fingernail tapped the wooden desk. Beneath it, her leg bounced.

"What about the mother?"

"Ivana Ressala," the doctor said.

Not his wife. "Can we reach her?"

An apologetic tone came through. "Her body was found a few days ago." He paused. Crinkling paper came over the phone. "It says here Ivana had a brother, might be worth looking into. It says he is in the service."

After their farewells, Olga stared out the window into the storm. She tried to imagine a baby lying out there in the cold for hours. She also tried to imagine someone leaving a baby to die.

Outside her office, staff shuffled back and forth, some of them ushering children, others carrying them on their hips. She gripped the bridge of her nose. Victor Kerensky was the largest known heroin supplier in Russia. Nobody knew yet his daughter was under their roof.

"Daddy. Who is that man in your office?

The perplexed look on her father's face. "He is an acquaintance of mine, who is beginning his political career soon. He came over for some advice."

The weasel looking man sipped from a snifter and puffed at a cigar. She stared at him through the crack in the door.

A little research proved her father wasn't lying. He had tried his hand at politics. His career was short lived, likely from corruption.

The stairs creaked beneath her weight as she made her way up. A couple of kids played peacefully in the hall, which earned them a grin. Standing before the nursery door, Olga wondered what she'd do. There were decisions to make. The safety of the orphanage depended on it.

Talc greeted her. A familiar scent. A long time ago, when she'd only been staff, Olga spent many hours in the nursery. She'd sung every lullaby and read every book they had a thousand times. Some of them she still remembered, verbatim.

With her back to Olga, Anna leaned over the crib with a binky in her hand.

Olga passed them and went to the window, but not without stealing a glance into the crib. "Beautiful, isn't it?"

Anna straightened and looked out the window. "Very."

It wasn't common for Olga to come into the nursery anymore. Usually, she spent most of her waking hours at her desk. There was always paperwork to do or phone calls to make. Judging by the look on her face, Olga knew she sensed something.

Anna asked, "Can I help you with something?"

Light streamed in from the window casting on her face. She turned to look at Anna. "I was just checking on you. Making sure you have everything under control." Olga glanced in the crib, hoping not to draw too much attention. Luckily, she didn't look much like her father.

Anna fetched a blanket from a chair. "Is there something bothering you?" She covered a baby. "Did I do something wrong?"

Instead of telling her the truth, Olga walked for the door. "It's been a long time since I've been up here. I wondered what you've done with the place." She ran her finger across the wallpaper. "It looks nice." With that, she left.

As she roamed the halls, laughter and footsteps called through the old house. Music to her ears. *The secret is just too big. It's just a matter of time before he finds out. She isn't safe here.*

Standing in the doorway, Olga observed Clarissa Dane. She served as staff and head of education. She was the most trustworthy person she had. As she worked, Olga watched. She'd made an excellent choice hiring the American woman.

Anna was a solid worker, too, but young and naïve.

A pit in her stomach warned her telling anyone was a mistake. Certainly, the secret could only grow, but she didn't think it was fair to keep it hidden either. After all, their safety could be jeopardized. Certainly, Clarissa would know what to do.

Olga crossed her arms. "When you have a second." She hiked a thumb over her shoulder.

Clarissa looked up from her activity book, smiling children on either side of her. "Of course, dear."

Their shoes clacked against the hardwood floor as they moved down the hallway. Olga intentionally led her away from the crowd. "I can't get into specifics right now, but Mishka can't stay here. We aren't safe with her under our roof."

Clarissa stopped, sandy brown hair settling on her shoulders. "Been doing a little digging around, have we?" She smirked. "I'm assuming the DNA results came back a match. The rumors are all over town."

Her stomach dropped. Throughout her entire career, she'd never dealt with anything like this. Plenty of disgruntled parents but none with resources like Kerensky. He had the power to shut them down for good.

Gripping the bridge of her nose, fighting back a headache, she asked, "Does he know she's here?"

Clarissa shook her head. "I don't think so, but it won't take long. If I'm already hearing it in my circles..."

Olga nodded.

A sneer crossed Clarissa's face. "I hate that bastard. He took my husband from me."

Once, when they'd gone out for drinks, Clarissa had told the story. It wasn't because of drugs but money. They'd fallen on hard times, and he'd taken a loan from the mafia. He didn't get back to work as quickly as planned, and the interest rates stacked up so fast. They never found his body.

Clarissa rested a hand on Olga's shoulder. "We'll talk later."

A journalist had once written a piece on Kerensky's connections. The rumors started circulating. Half a dozen officers denied involvement with him or the organized crime syndicates. Three days after the paper published the slanderous article, the journalist's house burned down. The fire department didn't arrive for four hours, claiming they were tending to other matters. No other fires were reported that night. Six weeks later the station had a brand-new truck.

Sitting in her office, holding a coffee cup with a shaking hand, Olga got on the phone with the military. She tried to track down Mishka's uncle. They told her he was on an assignment, and she would have to wait for his return. Olga had a hard time imagining this man giving up his career to take care of a little girl he'd likely never met.

CHAPTER Six

Kansas City, Missouri.

After several hours of negotiation, Mr. Forest decided not to press charges. There were circumstances, of course. Lester wasn't allowed to walk by his house. He'd have to take the long way home. He'd also have to resume counseling, which Virginia had already planned on. She agreed to all of his terms.

For one week she drove him back and forth. He'd already long since been kicked off the bus and her work proved to be far too demanding. A handful of times they went over his new path. If he got caught anywhere near Mr. Forest or Hercules, he'd pay the price.

The new path went down Main Street for a couple of blocks. At first, he didn't think he'd like that. He wasn't fond of people and there were plenty of them downtown, but he did like the storefront windows. As he walked, he couldn't help looking at all the displays. Occasionally he'd catch a glimpse of himself in the reflection and shudder.

He didn't look anything like Cory Hill, the most sought after of all the boys in their school. Cory had dark hair and a chiseled jaw. The girls didn't look at Lester the same way they looked at Cory. He also showed a lot of promise as an athlete. Lester had the hand-eye coordination of a drunk.

The news about Hercules had spread throughout the school. It didn't take long for Lester to piece together that Mr. Forest had a nephew a grade above him. From the moment he stepped inside, the kids looked at him differently.

Walking through the lobby, Lester saw Cory Hill coming. He avoided eye contact, pretended to be interested in something in the trophy case. It didn't stop Cory from knocking everything out of his hands and calling him a psycho.

Throughout the day, more rumors floated around. Their eyes were on him all the time. Their whispers followed him everywhere he went. As stories sometimes do, it morphed after many retellings. According to some of the rumors, he'd killed Hercules. According to others he'd painted his face with the dogs blood like *Lord of the Flies*.

A piece of square pizza sat untouched on his tray. With the knot in his stomach, he couldn't eat. Even if it was his favorite. He didn't dare take his eyes off the table. He'd always been an outcast, but it had gotten much worse. Everyone hated him. Even the teachers gave disapproving looks. He had no doubt there would be more vigilante justice.

Laura had turned her back on him, probably for good. That was the worst part. He'd disappointed her. All the chances of them holding hands or kissing went out the window. For that, he hated himself even more.

The bell blared throughout the school, releasing the children. Lester walked quickly, gripping his books tight to his chest.

He figured he'd slip through the courtyard and out the gate. There was always less traffic that way. They were waiting for him. Cory Hill and Jerry Morris stood by the gate. On sight, Cory cracked his knuckles.

Lester turned to run, but realized the audience blocked his way. They wouldn't let him escape. He had to pay the piper. Thunderous crashes of his heart pounded his ribcage. The urge to puke swept over him but he managed to swallow it back.

Cory moved closer. "Are you afraid?" The distance between them shrunk. "Aren't you going to come after me?"

With one hearty shove, Lester fell.

Wind escaped his lungs in a quick blast. Pain shot through his back and his legs. Cory stood over him. *They've all turned on me.* Although he anticipated problems, he didn't expect them so fast.

"Right. I'm not a defenseless animal," Cory sneered.

The circle tightened around him. "Get him, Cory!" someone screamed.

After scrambling in the dirt, Lester found his feet. The circle was airtight. He couldn't run away. He remembered the look of fear on those girls faces and a terrible smile curled his lip. The thirst for power overcame him.

Lester lunged at Cory, who sidestepped him. He tumbled past, nearly losing his balance.

The audience caught him and pushed him back into the center.

Cory snapped a right jab, which caught Lester in the nose, and his head jolted back. The pain made his eyes water. At first, he wasn't sure, but then he saw blood dripping on his shoes.

You're going to pay for this, Hill. You will pay.

The second slug caught him in the temple. A kaleidoscope of colors danced through closed eyelids. He wasn't crying from pain, but anger. Lester charged again and landed his first hit. The punch landed firmly on his cheekbone, knocking him off kilter.

They grappled.

"You're done picking on animals, psycho," Cory said. A choir of followers agreed.

Through gritted teeth, Lester muttered, "Fuck you."

Cory managed to get around him and caught him in a headlock.

With an arm slung around his neck, Lester didn't like the odds. He'd never been much of a fighter.

Lester's pulse fired like a cannon in his head. His attempts to break Hill's grip, failed. He struggled to breathe. His face crimson.

Lester managed to take it to the ground.

The two flopped around in the dirt. He had been in the headlock a long time, and the struggle slowed. He'd never been so exhausted in his life. Hill let go and pushed Lester away. The boy sprawled out on the dirt. He gasped. The color began returning to his face. A cloud of dust rose around him, signaling his defeat. He expected the crowd to kick him and rejoiced when they didn't.

Lester lay in the dirt, chest heaving. Spots danced in his vision. Feet tattered across the courtyard, as the audience dispersed. He hadn't done well. From the corner of his eye, he saw Laura. She looked disappointed. He didn't dare look up from the dirt again.

This isn't over yet. Far from it.

CHAPTER SEVEN

Serpukhov, Russia.

The little bundle of pink blankets laid still. Blue clouded wallpaper surrounded them. They'd convinced Anna to run to the store. It was the only way they could remove her from the nursery without raising more suspicion. Standing over the crib in the darkness, Olga couldn't help but feel terrible. She didn't want Mishka to go, but it wasn't safe for her to stay.

Clarissa planted a hand on Olga's shoulder. "They already know she's here. A guy came asking about her while I was at the laundromat yesterday."

It's just a matter of time before they break down the door. Although quite intimidating to the children, Olga stood no chance against the mafia. If they came armed, she didn't know what she could do to stop them. Even the police couldn't be trusted.

Clarissa's fingers laced through the boards of the crib. "Have you found out about the uncle yet?"

Their voices were whispers among sleeping babies. "He's on a mission."

Clarissa stepped away from the crib and turned to the window, moonlight lit her face. This light made her look older. "What are we going to do?"

Wind whipped snow off the roof. "There's nothing I can do for a few more weeks. Babies are hard."

Careful not to wake the children, they walked down to her office and closed the door. They got to work. Among her files, Olga kept a Rolodex of numbers for foster parents in the area. Some of them she hadn't talked to in years.

As they worked through the list, they began starting their conversations with, "Sorry it's late."

Olga had excluded all the locals. Mishka didn't stand a chance living close. If the rumors were already circulating, she didn't have much time.

Defeat covered both of their faces. "I called every number you gave me," Clarissa said.

Leaning an arm on her desk and gripping the bridge of her nose, Olga fought back tears. "I tried everyone I could think of, too."

The front door creaked open, causing them both to jump.

Although she couldn't see her, Olga remembered she'd sent Anna off to run an errand.

Clarissa leaned over and whispered, "Come by my place."

Olga needed to get away from the orphanage for a bit. Although part of her didn't want to leave. She considered that it might be dangerous to go. Perhaps they were already watching. She fought off these thoughts, promising she'd be careful.

Inside the kitchen Olga took one of the bags off the table and started working through it. Normally, one person wouldn't do the shopping, but these were special circumstances.

Judging by the look on her face, Anna knew something was up.

Standing in the quiet of the kitchen, Anna asked, "Is something wrong?"

Cans of corn and peas thumped on the shelves as Olga tried not to look at her. Tears lingered in the corner of her eyes. She couldn't hold back the secret any longer. It wasn't fair to keep her in the dark.

Unable to face her, Olga stared into the pantry. "The baby has to go."

Anna stopped what she was doing, set the box of pasta down on the table. "What baby?"

"Mishka."

CHAPTER EIGHT

Kansas City, Missouri.

The cafeteria filled with students who'd forgotten about Lester's savage beating. *Revenge.* From across the cafeteria, he glared at Cory Hill. The hatred hadn't gone away. They'd moved on but hadn't forgiven him. They treated him like a pariah, every day.

The nosey bitch who questioned him three days a week didn't know anything. He'd done a great job at feeding her enough bullshit to keep her busy.

As he walked past Cory, he fantasized about smashing the back of his head with the tray. The volume of the cafeteria made it difficult to eavesdrop. All he successfully heard was Cory mention going to his uncle's house for the weekend. He slammed his tray on the counter and walked back, listening more intently. Cory explained to his friend Jerry that his uncle lived nearby. Loch Lloyd.

That night he tossed and turned. The beating was still fresh in his mind. The others had forgotten, but not Lester. The words of the therapist circulated as he stared up at the ceiling. *"Holding onto your anger is like drinking poison and expecting the other person to die."*

Since the mess with Hercules, Lester's ability to sleep had faded. Mostly he watched the streetlights outside his window. They'd shoved more pills down his throat. A small pile of them had grown beneath his pillow and an even smaller pile behind the pipes under the sink.

With his fork, Lester rolled a sausage link around on his plate. His appetite had been as sparse as his sleep. When he did take all of the meds, they made him nauseous. The doctors claimed the feeling would go away when he adjusted, but he'd never given them that chance. When his mother watched, he took them. When she wasn't watching, he didn't.

He couldn't stand staring down at the plate a second longer and told his mother he'd be outside playing with the twins. Tricking her had never been difficult. He'd always enjoyed doing it, too. She didn't know he hadn't played with them in months. They, like all the other kids, wanted nothing to do with him.

Cars whizzed by. People spoke on cellphones. The buzz of a lawnmower filled the neighborhood, accompanied by the scent of freshly cut grass. To anyone else, they might have called it a perfect day. Not Lester. He was too busy drinking the metaphorical poison.

Hanging out with the twins hadn't even crossed his mind, except as a lie to his mother. If he had to hear about their dads porn stash in the garage one more time, he'd be sick. And, if he had to sit through them trading baseball cards again, he'd hang himself.

Lester found the road that led to Cory's house. He walked up and down the street, passing kids playing in yards. A mailbox said "Hill" on the front, and he figured it had to be the one. As he paced up and down the street, he tried to convince himself he only wanted to talk to Cory. The little voice inside wouldn't allow him to lie to himself. They were long past talking.

A noise came from the house, startling him. Quickly, Lester hid behind a car. He stole a glance across the hood as they stepped onto the porch. Father and son.

The man called back into the house. "What street?"

An unseen voice returned. "Birch Street."

Birch Street. Loch Lloyd.

Carrying a baseball glove in one hand and a red cap, Cory looked excited. They walked down the path of their beautiful suburban home and got into a nice car. The father gave him a loving smile, which made Lester sneer.

If they'd been alone, he would have gone after him. He'd find the biggest stick around and make him pay.

Loch Llyod proved to be one hell of a walk, but with anger boiling in his veins, he managed. Many times, he imagined that look of fear spread on Cory's face. Somewhere in the depths of his sadistic mind, he heard Cory begging for mercy.

The heat burned the top of his head. Sweat creased his brow. A low, miserable ache pounded at his heels. His tongue had long gone dry and several times he thought about stopping for water but carried on.

Mind over matter.

Two hours passed before Lester stared at a green street sign that said, *Birch.* The houses were nice. The sun above still shined heavily, letting him know he still had plenty of time. There weren't any houses with the name "Hill" on the mailboxes. No signs of Cory either.

Without a clue where to go, Lester circled the block. Something would come to mind. It always did.

An elderly couple stepped out of a garage with lawn chairs in hand. They sat, exchanging glances in Lester's direction. As soon as he noticed them, he became paranoid. *They know why I'm here. They set out those chairs to watch me.* He walked between two houses, attempting to get out of sight, feeling their eyes follow him.

A ragged buzz grew louder.

Behind one of the houses were Cory and his uncle tossing wood into a chipper. Lester crouched behind some shrubs. *Here you are, you little fucker.* They worked diligently, stopping long enough to wipe sweat or adjust their gloves. That stupid red baseball hat still covered his head.

A log thumped into the chute. "How much longer, Uncle Chuck?"

"The game doesn't start until three," he said.

Another piece clanked into the chipper. The engine hummed as it ground the log into bits. Chuck threw a piece in, too. It spat out shreds that landed into a small pile on the other side of the machine.

Sweat stains covered their chests, which led him to believe they'd been at it for a long time. Two hours according to Lester's watch.

As they worked, Lester searched the ground for a weapon. With only his fists, he'd never win. He'd tried that. A stick or a rock would suffice. That's when he stumbled upon a log.

Staring back at the woodpile, Chuck said, "C'mon. We still have a long way to go. Pick it up."

A little attitude came forth. "I know. I'm just really hot."

Judging by their bickering Chuck had agreed to take him to the game if he'd help. He went on for a little bit about the importance of a hard day's work and how it built character or some shit.

Chuck stopped for a second, wiping his brow. "Want some water?"

Cory looked at the pile with dread. Still a lot of wood left to chop. "Yeah, sure."

The door on the patio slid open and Chuck disappeared inside. Hair on the back of Lester's neck stood on end. The feeling of power came over him again. The insatiable thirst for fear and control coursed through his veins like a snakes venom.

With his back to Lester, Cory tossed wood into the chipper. The machines rumble covered the sound of his footsteps as he drew closer, keeping a keen eye on the door. It didn't take long before Lester had gotten right on top of him. His feet pounded the ground with every step.

Cory turned in time to see Lester charging with the log over his head. The wood fell from his arms and his jaw slacked open. He didn't have time to scream.

The log cracked against his head with a hideous thud. Cory stumbled, hand landing inside the chute. Wet, obnoxious gurgles escaped its mechanical teeth as he screamed. With each rotation, the woodchipper pulled him in further.

An opportunity to save his life presented itself, but Lester didn't take it. He had no interest in being a hero. All he wanted was to watch Cory suffer. It chewed, just loud enough to muffle his screams.

It didn't take long to fully consume the boy.

The screaming stopped, but the machine didn't.

Oh, my God, he's dead. I can't believe he's dead.

From between the houses, the uncle's shriek startled Lester. The neighbors had gone inside, and he bolted down the street, checking over his shoulder to assure he hadn't been seen.

There wasn't a feeling of guilt, not exactly. Concern about prison worried him, but even that wasn't that bad. The thrum of his heart pressed into his ears as he raced away. Certainly, he'd be the main suspect. He hated the kid, and everyone knew it.

To say that he wasn't capable of any emotions wasn't completely true. He felt something. An unfamiliar strange feeling. Loss? Remorse? He pondered it as he slid into a small park and sat down on a swing.

Sitting on a swing, listening to police sirens fill the neighborhood, he contemplated what he'd do if he got away with it. He wondered if he'd do it again. He wondered if he'd turn his life over to the lord, like they pushed for in school. He even considered getting back on the medication.

CHAPTER NINE

Serpukhov, Russia.

Olga walked around the house, locking all the windows. She'd always wanted a security system but couldn't afford one. The government subsidies weren't enough and apparently, they didn't care about the children's safety that much.

Under ordinary circumstances, she'd oppose a gun, but it was life or death. As if having a mobsters daughter under her roof wasn't bad enough, she didn't know who she could trust. There were too many officers on his payroll.

A can of pepper spray had sat in the bottom of her purse for so long she wondered if it still worked. On the opposite side of the house, Clarissa Dane made similar inspections. They were looking out the windows for strange cars, checking for footsteps in the snow around the property.

At some point they were going to have to tell the children. Sooner rather than later. Olga had been on the phone with other orphanages trying to unload Mishka on them. They all said they weren't taking any more infants. It wasn't fair to lie to them either. If they didn't know, it could be detrimental.

Several times over the last few days she'd snuck off to cry. She didn't want anyone to know. The kids didn't need the added pressure and although the other workers were understanding, she didn't want them to see her like that. A strong composure made them all feel safe.

After fixing her makeup numerous times, Olga decided not to wear any. There were too many tears for that.

The flint of a lighter scratched in the dark, fire wiggled as she tried to light the cigarette. The cherry lit and she inhaled deeply, hoping it would soothe her nerves. A plume of smoke blew from her lips before the phone rang.

They didn't receive many calls late at night. A chill ran her blood cold. She imagined Kerensky on the other line, waiting to talk to her.

The familiar yet timid voice of the old man who'd brought Mishka in surprised her.

"They've been here. They destroyed our home." A hysterical woman wept in the background.

CHAPTER TEN

Kansas City, Missouri.

Virginia called from the bottom of the stairs. "Lester, honey come down here."

He'd been hiding in his room for hours, waiting for someone to figure it out.

No police officers were visible, which came as a relief.

She held the phone to one ear. "Hold on a second, Penelope," she said, shifting the phone against her shoulder. "Lester, please sit down." When there was bad news, she always made him sit. "Did you know Cory Hill? He goes to your school."

"Yeah, I know him," he said quietly. The thoughts began to race. *Leave everything. You can make it if you only RUN!* Lester tried to reason with himself, tried to calm himself, perhaps they still didn't know anything. People got away with murder sometimes.

Her voice softened, so did her demeanor. "There was a terrible accident last night. He passed away." Again, she shifted the phone.

Accident?

The memory of Cory hanging from the woodchipper returned. He swallowed back the acidic bile working its way up his throat. There'd been blood everywhere. The red cap had been lying on the ground... Accident?

After hanging up, she rubbed his back like she'd done when he was a toddler. "Was that one of your buddies?"

"Yeah," he lied. "Same math class and stuff." He acted as if he missed him. The sympathetic face he put on was nothing more than a rouse. Deep inside, the cogs turned. The seed of corruption soiled, and he got away with it.

If they were going to come for me, it would have happened by now.

She ran her fingers through his hair, another thing she'd stopped doing since he'd grown bigger. Her attempts to comfort him were genuine and even sweet. He portrayed emotions he'd picked up from TV. The sad, depressed face of someone mourning. The vacant stare of disbelief. The complex look of grief and misery. He alternated them, mimicking as best he could. No matter how hard he tried, he couldn't produce tears. The mirror had helped him improve at acting.

In the gymnasium were two blown up pictures of Cory Hill. Lester grimaced at them, remembering the look of confusion and fear only seconds before he died. The principle rambled about how tragic it was and how they should never lose a child. She also explained that there would be help for those who needed it. The school had brought in a couple of grief counselors, and they'd be around for a week or so.

Throughout the day, Lester kept his head down. The last thing he wanted to do was draw attention to himself. They hadn't figured out his involvement. In fact, they didn't even know he was there. The uncle didn't see him run off.

Mourning children moped about the school, crying in bursts. Outside his locker were a bunch of flowers. People had also stuck Post-it notes on the door with loving messages.

The principal stopped him in the hallway and asked him to follow her to her office. Together they walked along the halls, saying nothing. A couple of times he wondered if she knew. Judging by her relatively calm demeanor, he didn't think so.

Lester nearly jumped out of his skin when the door slapped shut. He couldn't help laughing at himself because of how silly it was.

She dropped her body weight into the chair with an oomph. Her nails tattered on the desk like pebbles on ice. "Do you know why I brought you in here?"

He shook his head.

"I know you're prone to acting out under stress. I'm begging you, please, not now." She spoke calmly. "If you need some time off to cope, I can arrange a couple of days. The last thing I need is you in trouble on top everything going on here." The large woman glared at him, expecting an answer. Her face was stern. It wasn't a look that said she'd take any of his crap. Not like she had before. The look said anguish and grief. Lester knew if he acted out, she'd send him packing, probably for good.

He guessed she'd already ran the idea by his mother.

With the memories fresh in his mind, Lester didn't want to be alone. When he closed his eyes, he could still see his feet hanging from the chute. The grinding noise from the chipper haunted him.

He shook his head, trying to free himself from the memories. "I won't be bad."

A questioning look came over her face. "Do you need to talk to the counselor? If so, she's here for another couple of hours."

Again, he shook his head.

Stepping out into the hallway, he tried to shake the feeling that had overwhelmed him. Could it be guilt? It certainly wasn't something he'd felt before. Whatever it was, it had shaken him. Seeing all those sad people bothered Lester.

Although he didn't want to admit it, the death had changed him. Something inside felt dirty. He'd committed the most unforgivable sin and at such a young age, too.

Lester stopped in front of the guidance counselor's office. The place the counselor had set up shop. He stared at the door, unsure if he could enter or not. The silver hair of a woman shone through the crack. His heart picked up. He stared blankly at the door. *What if I go in, only for a moment? What if I tell her I felt bad because we fought, and we never made up?*

Before he could knock, it opened. His jaw fell. An older woman with big gaudy teeth stared down at him. "Hello, Lester," she said.

How did you know my name?

She stepped aside. "Come in, please. Your principal has told me about you."

His eyes cast to the floor.

The seat crackled under her weight. "Were you and Cory close?"

His sneakers chirped at the tile as he slid his foot back and forth. "Not really, no. We got into a big fight. We never got the chance to make up, before, before…" He couldn't finish. Lester bit harshly into his lip, trying to refrain from telling. Blood pooled in his mouth, stopping behind his teeth. If he hadn't bit his lip, the words would have jumped out.

Leaning back, chewing on a pen, she said, "I bet he would have forgiven you. Kids get into quarrels all the time. It's part of growing up." Mrs. Danforth extended a sympathetic hand. She didn't notice the grimace in his face as he sunk his teeth further into his lip, biting back the secret.

For a little while the counselor dug, but he wouldn't let her get any further. He'd already been well versed in stalling with his regular therapist.

She placed the tissue box on the desk. "It's tragic when they go so young," she added. "A little girl came in here earlier, nearly hysterical because now Cory won't be her husband when they grow up."

Laura, he thought distantly. A part of him knew, deep down. He'd known all along.

"What do we do now?"

Her wrinkled hands came together in her lap. "We never forget."

Walking out turned into a jog, which became a run.

Never forget? The echo of his feet against the pavement rang through his head. Never forget? The image of Cory hanging from the woodchipper had been seared into his mind. He didn't think he could forget. Franklin Street turned into Dover, and he kept running.

Instead of forgetting, Lester tried to justify it. Cory had instigated things. *He was the one who was pushing me around. He deserved it.* A chill ran through him, like ice water in his veins. From that moment on, he'd never be the same.

There's something wrong with me. He'd always been filled with bad thoughts, ones he couldn't suppress. If unstifled, those bad thoughts turned into bad actions. The evil spread through him, venom from a snake bite.

Musty smelling boxes cluttered the back of the garage. Redemption ran through his mind as he pushed aside Pokémon cards and old clothes. After pawing through them for twenty minutes, he found what he'd been looking for. The Bible.

He didn't want to have those wicked thoughts anymore. He'd grown tired of being known as the bad kid and wondered if it was too late.

The image of Cory persisted, keeping him up late at night. Sometimes he'd think about it for days on end. Sometimes he'd even think about doing it again. He couldn't deny he felt alive when it happened, something he didn't feel often. There was something... exhilarating about the kill. No matter how unforgivable.

CHAPTER ELEVEN

Serpukhov, Russia.

All the children gathered in the nursery under Anna's watchful eye. The phone call was upsetting. The thugs were looking for her and it was only a matter of time before they came knocking, or worse... not.

A single desk lamp illuminated the office. In the dim lighting Clarissa looked nervous. Although Olga felt it, she couldn't show it. She had a reputation to keep. She had to be a fearless leader for the children.

Looking up from the clutter of foster parent profiles and phone numbers, Clarissa said, "I got you something."

Their eyes met. "What's that?"

Contents rattled inside her purse as Clarissa retrieved a silver flask. She shook it a couple of times with a wide smile. The liquor sloshed about.

Olga's face turned up for a second before she took it.

Pressing it to her lips, Olga drank. The ice cold vodka burned her throat and hurt her teeth. "How did you get it so cold?"

A smile crossed her face. The first smile in a long time. "I left it in the snowbank by my car. I was planning on drinking it after work, but we need it now."

Through the cracked door, they saw the dark hallway beyond. "I love this place," Olga whispered.

Clarissa tipped back the flask. "I can see why. There's a certain type of magic here."

She took the flask back. "My heart breaks every time one comes in… and every time one leaves. I have been doing this for fifteen years. I've seen some awful things, but this is one of the worst. This and Galina Fleming." Olga's eyes turned to the door as if just saying her name were painful.

Clarissa stole a glance at the hallway, as if they were exchanging dark secrets. "Who is Galina Fleming?"

"Nearly ten years ago a little girl came in around the age of thirteen. I knew she was a victim. She showed all the signs. Something convinced me it was the father. How were we to know? The state won custody but turned it over to her mother after she proved herself worthy. Six months went by, and Galina came back. She stopped going to therapy. When she came back this time, things were worse."

The wind pressed against the windows.

Clarissa tipped back the flask, draining the last drop. "What happened?"

"Turns out, Galina's mother had been cheating. Stepdad was sneaking into her room at night." Olga's eyes met the floor. She took a pause, emotions running high.

The cap of the flask screwed on and off as Clarissa stared in horror. "Oh no."

A tear stood in the corner of her eye. "She wasn't in our care for more than three days when it happened. It was about four in the morning. I stayed the night, watching the house. I walked down the hall to the staircase. I couldn't see in the dark, but something tapped me on the shoulder." She shook her head. "She hung herself from the banister in the hall. It was her shoe that tapped me." A tear escaped Olga's eye. "I can't walk through that hall without remembering. I did everything I could." Olga wiped at the tears streaming down her face.

A knock interrupted the silence and Olga's heart free fell.

Their footfalls echoed in the empty hallway. Olga's legs trembled with every step. They stood there, staring at each other, trying to gain their composure. They knew it would happen, but they hadn't managed to steal themselves.

The door creaked open, revealing two men fighting off the cold.

Thugs.

Olga looked them over disapprovingly. "Can I help you, gentlemen?"

As the smaller of the two spoke, he tried stealing glances over her shoulder. "Um, I was wondering if I could um, adopt a child."

That was a half-assed excuse if she'd ever heard one. "Sorry to inform you, fellas, but we're closed. Come back later."

Before she could close the door, he blocked it with his foot. "You don't want us to come back." The pitch in his voice changed. "You know why we're here."

Trying to contain the tremble in her voice, Olga said, "You're too late."

The thug chuckled.

The quiet one sneered.

Removing his foot from the doorway he said, "Alright, we'll do it the hard way."

The door slammed in their faces, followed by the loud clunk of the lock. Olga held a finger to her lips, trying to keep quiet until they were gone. Beneath the surface a scream bubbled.

Their footsteps echoed through the long hallway and up the stairs. Adrenaline poured through Olga's veins as she climbed them two at a time. It had been a long time since she'd walked that fast, even longer since she'd felt her heart flailing about.

Together they waved Anna out of the nursery and into the hall. Once the door closed, they began their chat. There wasn't much to say except the truth. The whole thing. Once she'd finished catching Anna up to speed, Olga decided.

"Mishka leaves tonight."

CHAPTER
TWELVE

Drexel, Missouri.

Lester Klass checked himself into Drexel City Mental Hospital. Ten years of uninterrupted madness had brought him to the brink of insanity. His shrink tried everything she could to medicate and comfort him, but he told her nothing. He couldn't, not even with the doctor/patient confidentiality. The medication didn't help. It only made him nauseous, like it had during his childhood. When on the medication, Lester didn't feel like himself. He lived in a terrible fog.

Ten years hadn't gotten him any closer to a girlfriend, or any friends at all. Some of them never forgot about the incident with Hercules and the others just didn't like him. The red hair and freckles made him stand out, but his lack of hygiene and poor outlook on life made him insufferable. He'd only found one friend, the Lord and Savior.

His therapist had convinced him to check into the hospital, which he'd fought tooth and nail at first. She'd offered to call his mother, which he also denied. It'd been too long. Even if he wanted to talk to her, he wasn't sure she'd want to talk to him.

Springs hissed as he sat on the edge of the bed. Orderlies spoke outside the door, pacing back and forth, peddling meds to crazy people.

When the man in the next room wasn't screaming through the night, he often talked to himself. Lester asked numerous times to move, but they wouldn't allow it. Because he was there by choice, he didn't have the same freedoms or rights the others did.

A worn Bible sat on the nightstand. Dogeared and beaten, but still as reliable as the day he'd taken it out of the garage. Every day since Cory's death had been a test and he treated them as such. He hadn't killed again, but the urge returned. Other urges surfaced, too.

At night, while his neighbor pounded his head off the wall, he read passages. Prayer often stifled his evil thoughts.

The nauseous feeling he got after taking his medication swept over him. A picture of Jesus hung on the wall, and he tried to remember scripture. When he needed them most, they'd be there. If only his memory were a little better.

An orderly in white scrubs entered, holding a tray of meatloaf and mashed potatoes. A whiff of her perfume sparked a fire within. He'd never been with a woman and thought about it endlessly. Lust. His nights were lonely, and the Bible couldn't save him from the expression of himself. She wasn't the most attractive woman, but the prettiest orderly the mental hospital had to offer. A couple of times she'd almost caught him in the act.

Raven hair hung on her shoulders. Large breasts protruded from the uniform shirt. Too much makeup covered her face, which bothered him. He thought she might look better without it. Routinely he tried to talk to her, to really talk to her. He'd try to make conversation, to get to know her. She would only go so far. He suspected she knew he liked her.

Rose didn't like him in any romantic fashion. That didn't stop him from entertaining some interesting ideas. When they did talk, she always brought up why she'd gotten into the field. She had a brother with schizophrenia. She'd taken care of him when they were younger and thought she could apply those skills in the workforce.

Lester accepted the tray with a gracious smile. He considered sparking a conversation with her, but the waves of nausea were too much. Gripping his stomach and staring at the tray, he thought he might hurl. The food in the hospital wasn't good, especially the meatloaf, which tasted like Styrofoam drenched in grease.

Thud. Thud. Thud.

His neighbor slammed his head against the wall. He was under constant supervision, which meant orderlies came and went around the clock. There'd been talk about getting him a helmet and threats of restraints, but they'd never followed through. Lester could hear everything through the thin wall.

Clutching the book, Lester attempted to read the parables. He'd already gone through it three times. Parts of it didn't make sense and he sought answers. Also, he tried adjusting the book to follow his will. Kane had slain Abel after all.

Thud, thud, thud.

The urges circulated in his mind. Another test. Aloud, Lester projected the good word, trying to block out the noise from the other side of the wall. The bad thoughts amplified.

"Ephesians 4:22-24. You were taught, about your former way of life, to put off your old self, which is being corrupted by its deceitful desires."

The thudding stopped.

Silence filled the void as he pressed his finger to the page. He'd been about to restart when a subtle knock came at the door. Before he could answer, Rose pulled it open. She collected his tray, half-eaten meatloaf still sitting in a cold, dry heap.

Setting down the Bible, he asked, "What's the story on the fella next door?"

She looked as if she could see right through the wall. "Max?" One finger pointed. "Well, he was a truck driver."

Lester nodded. "What did he do to end up here?"

A smirk crossed her face before she stole a glance at the door. "You know I'm not supposed to talk about that stuff."

Using his best attempt at charm, Lester pleaded. "C'mon. You can tell me."

Rose closed the distance to the door. At first, he thought she was going to walk out. Instead, she pushed it closed. "Promise you're not going to say a word?"

Using his finger, Lester crossed his heart.

The bedsprings creaked beneath her weight as she sat at the end. "Well, the story goes like this. He was making a trip up to Maine. He brought his two kids with him, and the weather had turned to shit, a really bad snowstorm. Up there, I guess they call them nor'easters." She shrugged. "The truck broke down on the side of the road and they were stranded. Nobody knows how or why, but he snapped."

A curious look crossed his face, involuntarily.

She continued. "When the police found him, the two kids were dead. Allegedly they found blood on his shirt and all over his hands. According to the story I found online, he ate them."

Stunned, they sat in silence. Lester tried to wrap his head around it. There were a lot of things going through his mind. The devil was hard at work both with Max and him.

She gave him a serious look, as if contemplating that she'd made a mistake. "He thinks God talks to him now..." She shook her head in pity.

As she bent over to collect the tray, Lester couldn't resist staring down her shirt. All the thoughts of sin came flooding back in. Even before she left the room, the blood had already started redirecting itself. Tatters of the story she'd told bounced around in his mind. Lester had thought about a lot of fucked up things, but cannibalism was a bridge too far, even for him.

They were called down to group.

Sitting in the circle, he looked around at all the helpless people, many of them addicts. All of them were there because they were struggling with something. He didn't know if they'd gone through the same things he had. Their stories were always entertaining.

Endlessly he'd hear about people stealing from their grandmother so they could get high or shooting up on their kids birthday. During this time, Lester's imagination ran wild, guilt free. He tried to put himself in their shoes, imagining what it was like to live. To truly live, not just wait around to die.

A woman with skin beaten by the sun, stood. Wrinkles had covered the circumference of her face. She looked like a woman who'd gone through hell and back. "Hello, everyone."

"Hello," they chanted back in unison.

That part always made Lester uncomfortable. It reminded him of a cult or something. He wondered how long before they were all shaving their heads and worshipping Xenu.

"My name is Denise." She paused, running ragged hands through thin hair. "I sold my body for drugs."

The visual of Denise lying on her back under some sweaty guy came to mind. He shook his head, trying to free himself from the thought. Not even an ounce of intrigue came with that one. Her complexion looked more like beef jerky than skin.

Repulsion came over him, followed by anger and disgust. He'd always hated prostitutes and couldn't figure out why.

The anger grew inside as he stared, unblinking. Even though her turn had ended, he couldn't stop staring. He couldn't stop thinking about it. Certainly, she'd committed many sins. Part of him was furious.

As the next person started their story, Lester chewed his nails. It wasn't until he'd bit into the nailbed and drawn blood that he noticed he'd been so aggressive.

The third person stood. He began with, "Hello, my name is Drew." That was all Lester heard from that guy because he got up and left.

He couldn't stay any longer. The urge to kill had come back full force. He wanted to do so much worse to her than he'd done to Cory. The woodchipper wasn't good enough. A hands on approach sounded much better.

In the center of the hall stood a ladder. A silver, glimmering ladder extended to the ceiling. A custodian stood three prongs up, replacing a bulb. The man stopped, pulled a handkerchief from his pocket, and blew his nose. Lester watched. The custodian didn't notice him. Protruding from his toolbelt was a screwdriver, which Lester swiped on his way by.

In the silence of the bedroom, he pulled the door closed. Exhilaration swept over him in waves. His fingers caressed the handle before he slid it under the mattress. If they caught him with it, they'd kick him out immediately. That would ruin his plans.

Lying with springs pressing into his back, Lester basked in the feeling of power. None of the other patients had a screwdriver. They weren't as sneaky or dangerous. Memories of Hercules came and with them that resurgence of power and frustration. The feeling was nothing short of intoxicating.

With his ear pressed to the door, Lester listened. The sun had gone down, and the people had gone quiet. During the day they were a rowdy bunch, but around nine o'clock they were as good as dead. Certain the coast was clear, he slid under the bed.

Plaster and paint fell as he chipped away at the wall. After what felt like three hours, pain shot throughout his wrist. Many times, he thought someone would walk in and catch him. With an eye to the door, he worked diligently until he'd formed a hole straight through to the other side.

Pressing his eye to it, he saw the bottom of the bed and two bare feet.

This is it.

In a deep voice, Lester spoke. "Max, I'm calling upon you to do my will."

Silence.

"Yes, God."

CHAPTER THIRTEEN

Sitting on the spiral staircase, ear pressed to the wall, Mishka listened. They were talking about her. They were always talking about her. At ten, she didn't understand everything they said. She didn't know what *mafia* meant. They often mentioned someone named Kerensky, who she assumed had been in the orphanage she'd come from. The way they spoke about him, he sounded like a bad man.

Kids played in the activity room at the top of the stairs. An airduct in the hall amplified the sounds, which worked perfectly for snooping. She wished they'd talk *to* her rather than *about* her. They didn't speak about the other kids like they did about her.

In order to get through her days, Mishka spent time thinking about the only friend she'd ever had. Anna. A beautiful blonde woman from the other orphanage. Once in a while she'd show up, always with treats.

Mishka wished she could live with her. Many times, she'd asked about it, but she always said no. *"It's too dangerous."* Aside from the janitor Mr. Golubev, Anna was the only person who was nice to her.

When there wasn't an adult present, the others teased her mercilessly. It wasn't uncommon for them to steal her food, hide her things, or call her names. They often said things like she'd never get adopted and that nobody loved her. Half of the children there knew their parents and they were in some custody battle or close to adoption. Not Mishka.

The closest she'd ever gotten was a phone call with an uncle she'd never met. He swore he'd take her when he could. Even that seemed like a lifetime ago. He swore after his military service they'd move far away.

In her wildest dreams, her uncle would meet Anna and they'd fall in love. They'd marry and then they'd all live happily together where all of her questions would have answers. And she wouldn't go hungry because there wouldn't be any other kids to steal her food.

Their murmured voices bounced off the air duct walls.

The door swung open, and Anna stepped inside. Mishka shot up and ran to her with arms wide open. Anna scooped her up and held her. She smelled of flowers, as she often did.

Nuzzling her head into Anna's shoulder, she asked, "When are you going to take me away from here?"

The smile faded. "Every time you ask me that, you break my heart a little more. I'm doing everything I can. I promise."

From her pocket came a little brown package. Mishka ripped it open revealing a tart with blueberry jam. Shreds of the wrapper laid on the floor and blueberry jam covered her mouth.

Anna took her by the shoulders. "Mishka. I need you to understand something."

The tart disappeared in the final bite.

"You won't remember her, but a woman who helped take care of you at the other place... died."

A look of surprise and sorrow crossed her face. "I'm sorry." Mishka wrapped her arms around Anna.

Tears welled in Anna's eyes. "There's more."

Mishka wanted to wipe away the tears.

Anna sniffled. "I think you're old enough now to understand. There are bad men out there. Bad men who could hurt you. That's why it's important to always be with an adult."

Mishka's lip trembled.

Anna wrapped her up in a big hug. "Those bad men hurt Olga."

The tears she'd been fighting started.

Anna wiped at them. "Now, we've come to the good news. Your uncle is finishing up his service and we're going to send you to be with him. He's going to take care of you and keep you safe."

Mishka stiffened. "Are you coming?"

Another hug.

"That's the part that hurts the most." She shook her head. "You're going to America. I have to stay here."

Together they cried. Anna tried to comfort her, but Mishka wanted no part of it.

As she sat on the stoop watching Anna climb into her car, she wondered what it would be like in America. She didn't know much about it, only what she'd seen on TV. All she could do was hope that her uncle was a nice man who'd love her because nobody ever had.

Maybe he will like the same things as me. She imagined them working side by side in the kitchen, music playing on the radio. *We can bake cookies.*

Anna drove away, promising out the window she'd fix everything when she came back.

CHAPTER
FOURTEEN

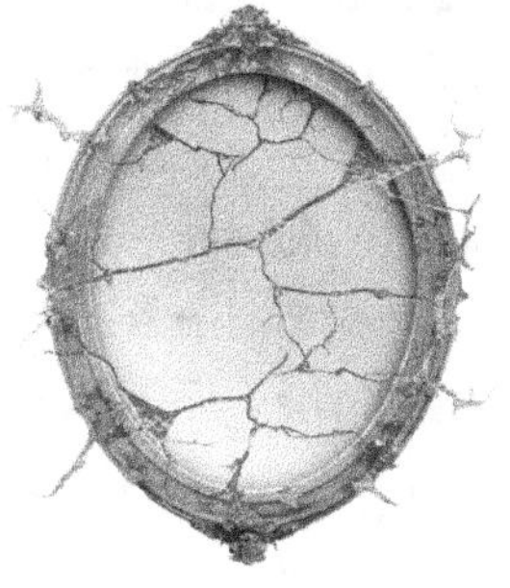

Drexel, Missouri.

A shout of terror rang through the halls of the mental hospital. Lester pulled himself out of bed and sprang for the door. At the end of the corridor a sea of people blocked the path. He pushed through the crowd.

Max held a knife to Denise's throat. A small group surrounding them, watched in horror. Orderlies edged closer, hoping to disarm him.

Sweat trickled from his forehead. "God told me to."

The knife glimmered in the light, pressing a groove into her flesh. The excitement nearly made Lester hard. She'd pay for her sins, just as he'd planned.

Wildly he swung the knife, hoping to deter the men inching closer. "I'll do it! Back off!"

The look of terror in Denise's eyes was exhilarating. He wished he had a camera to capture that look. He watched idly, trying to conceal the smile growing on his face. She pleaded with Max to let her go. Her jagged, desperate voice cut through the room like butter.

Again, he pointed the knife at the crowd. "I have to!" he shouted.

The orderlies backed away with their hands raised. A group of people had him surrounded, but he wasn't backing down. Pictures that had once hung on the wall lay on the floor, trampled.

"It's his will."

Max dragged the blade across her throat, and blood poured out. Everyone gasped. A couple of men pounced on him. The others leapt to help her. Her lifeless body thumped on the tile floor.

Amidst the chaos, Lester broke for the door. The guard station was empty. Walking out, he considered turning around for his things before thinking better of it. Even if they found the hole in the wall, they wouldn't put two and two together. Aside from his Bible, he only had a handful of clothes.

Stealing glances over his shoulder, Lester moved through the mobbed streets. Sirens blared, and it reminded him more of New York than Drexel. Cars splashed in puddles as they whizzed past.

A light drizzle came down on him as he crossed the street, stealing glances over his shoulder. *Why did I do that?* The passerby's beady eyes watched him in as he passed. Their stares made him feel guilty, as if they knew what he'd done.

A neon sign glimmered in the window of a rundown bar. He didn't drink much, but he couldn't ignore the smell of something on the grill. Also, he wanted to get out of the rain.

The adrenaline and other chemicals fired in his brain as he swung open the door, relishing his accomplishment. He rode that high as he walked through the joint.

A jukebox bumped from the corner, followed by the cracking of pool balls. A light buzz of chatter came from the bar itself. Lester walked closer, amused by the crowd. Shortly after the door closed, the rain poured.

They weren't looking at him like the people on the street. In fact, most of them didn't even notice him. The music vibrated in his shoes as he moved closer to the bar, fearful something might happen.

A beautiful woman with dark hair slung drinks. A young man straddled a barstool, staring into an empty rocks glass. Lester double checked his pocket, assuring himself he had enough to eat. He did.

The stool squeaked an uncomfortable noise as he climbed on it. The man only glanced at him before resuming his intense stare into the bottom of his glass.

With a rag slung over her shoulder, the bartender approached. "How can I help you, handsome?"

Lester didn't have the constitution for alcohol. He'd learned that about himself. A couple of drinks would make him into a monster. Not only would he be an asshole, but he couldn't handle it well and almost always threw up. Not to mention he didn't like the lack of control. Drunk, he said things he didn't want to say.

Handsome? She's only being polite, right? Right?

He snagged the menu but didn't really look at it. "Ginger ale and a burger. Rare."

She nodded and turned to Lester's counterpart. "What about you?"

He met her gaze. "Yeah, I'll take another." The glass scratched the counter as he pushed it closer to her.

With their orders, and his glass, she disappeared.

The man looked over and asked, "Is the food here any good?"

Lester shrugged. "I have no idea, first time."

He nodded. "Are you from around here?"

Muscles in his face tightened as he remembered how much he didn't like small talk. He fought off the grin and tried to be polite. "I was staying up the street." *At a fucking mental hospital,* he thought but didn't say. "It's for work."

A glass thumped on the bar in front of him. "What is it you do for work?"

He wondered if he'd backed himself into a corner. "Truck driver."

He'd concluded that if the man asked further, he'd say it was in a shop nearby. Luckily, he didn't.

As the burger and fries landed on the counter, Lester couldn't help but thinking about Denise. He could see that look in her eyes as she took her final breath. The gurgling sound she'd made. Cold ginger ale trickled down his throat, just as the blood had trickled toward his sneakers.

As his teeth sunk into the warm meat, images flashed through his mind. He imagined himself stabbing the bartender in the abdomen, listening to her squeal. He could almost hear her begging for her life. That's when he accepted that it would be more satisfying to do it himself. Pulling back from his bite, he witnessed blood dripping onto his plate and grinned.

CHAPTER FIFTEEN

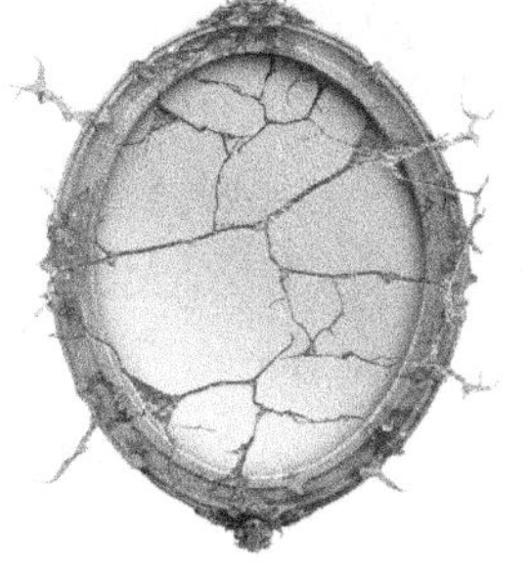

Rybinsk, Russia

Mishka sat on the orphanage stairs with her packed bags. She couldn't wait outside. That was against the rules, but they did allow her to sit in view of the door. Kids played at the top of the stairs. She wouldn't miss them. In fact, she didn't even want to say goodbye.

In her ten years in their care, she'd never gained any friends. She'd always been excluded from the games and chatter. The other kids didn't like her, but Mishka proved to be a worthy student. She took her education seriously and had outshined most of her classmates.

The time had finally come for her to meet the uncle she'd heard so much about. Part of her had grown concerned. *What if he doesn't like me? What if I end up in an orphanage in America?*

Although she never said it aloud, all she wanted was to be wanted.

Deep down Mishka hoped that Anna would adopt her. She'd swoop in at the last second and take her. The last saving grace. That hadn't happened and many nights Mishka laid in bed wondering why. She'd also shed a fair number of tears because of it.

The two men who ran the orphanage had gone back and forth for days. She'd listened to them through the vents. They'd said that the bad men would come for her. They were quite angry at Anna for not letting them know sooner. Mishka couldn't imagine why bad men would hurt a little girl.

Have I done something wrong?

For days Mishka wondered if she'd cry when the time came. As she sat on the steps, waiting for Anna to whisk her away, not a single tear came forth. She couldn't wait to leave. She wouldn't miss any of them, not the janitor Mr. Golubev. Not her roommate either.

A boy named Dimitri came down the hallway and stopped beside her. "You mean to tell me someone wants *you*?" A sneer crossed his face.

Her brow furrowed. "As a matter of fact-"

Before she could give him her thoughts, he kicked her bags down the stairs. They scattered and all of her clothes burst out like a popped balloon. Gathering her stuff, she turned to scream at him, but he'd already left.

Stuffing her clothes back in the bag, someone spoke from behind her.

"Oh, Mishka."

Goosebumps rose on her arms when she mistakenly thought it was her mother. Part of her imagined she'd turn up, looking for her and that she'd recognize her immediately. Then, she'd feel complete.

When she turned, Anna knelt beside her to help. "Are you okay?"

The tears she hadn't shed for leaving the orphanage lingered in her eyes. That felt like the closest she'd ever been to her mother, and she had to strain to keep them in.

Once her belongings were situated in the back seat of Anna's car, they were on the road. She drove a bit recklessly. A worried look creased her face. Every few minutes, Anna checked the mirror. Once or twice Mishka did, too, wondering what she was looking for.

They were running out of time. If she wanted to ask the burning questions, she'd have to do it quickly. It took a little while to bring them all into words.

In a moment of sheer bravery, Mishka asked, "Are you my mother?"

Anna stole a glance from the corner of her eye. "Oh, Mish. I wish more than anything that I were, but no."

A long pause fell between them.

Mishka crossed her arms. "You could be."

Another pause.

Anna closed her eyes for a second. "It's not safe enough for that."

Mishka stared out the window. "Why do they want me?"

"I can't…"

The dam that held back her tears, finally broke. "What did I do?"

Brakes screeched as Anna veered off the road. Her arms wrapped around Mishka. "Oh, honey, you didn't do anything. This isn't your fault."

Mishka pulled away. "It certainly feels that way."

In her arms, Mishka felt safe. Even if it wasn't for much longer.

For the remainder of the trip, Mishka stared out the window at passing trees. She didn't ask any more questions, she couldn't. Tears came and went, most of them she tried hiding from Anna, who'd already shed some of her own.

The car stopped and they ran toward the building where someone in uniform stopped them. Anna showed them identification and spoke really fast. He wasn't in a hurry like her. He moved like molasses.

Anna dragged her by the hand through revolving doors, which scared her at first. She wondered what would happen if they got stuck inside. When she noticed Anna wasn't the least bit afraid, she soldiered on.

Once inside, Mishka looked around. She'd never seen that many people. They were moving so quickly, dragging luggage behind them. As they progressed through the impossibly large building, Anna tugged at her hand. Mishka couldn't help staring at all the people and all the stuff. It was a whole different world from the orphanage.

Tugging back, Mishka asked, "How will I know it's him?"

Without looking, Anna asked, "What?"

She tugged again, trying to get her attention. "How will I know he's my uncle and not some stranger?"

Anna stopped at a desk, shoveling money into a woman's hand. "I sent him a picture of you. He will find you. Besides, the nice people at the other airport are going to help."

Standing in a long corridor with a single door at the end, Anna wiped away tears. She knelt down, wrapped Mishka in a huge hug. "I want you to know something, Mishka. I love you and what I'm doing is best for you."

The single door opened, and a woman stepped out. She didn't say anything, only held out a hand for Mishka to take. Together they walked through the door.

Before it closed, Mishka hollered over her shoulder, "I love you, Anna."

Wiping at the tears that streaked her face, Mishka stole one last glance at Anna before the door slammed shut.

CHAPTER
Sixteen

Drexel, Missouri.

A crackle came through the phone followed by his mother's judgmental voice. "Truck driving school?"

He tapped his fingers on his leg. "School is just the beginning. I'd like to go over the road. I'd work alone and control my own hours for the most part."

Silence met him on the other end of the line. He wasn't sure if she heard, or even if she cared. All throughout his life she'd doubted him. Not this time. Any negativity would be met with the dial tone. He'd never been more certain of anything in his life.

After finishing up the call, Lester dialed his therapist, who'd been helping him get into school. An eagerness crept inside unlike anything he'd felt since childhood. Memories of Christmas mornings long past came and went.

Trying to fight off the smile, Lester asked, "Is everything good?"

She concurred. "Yes, all of your paperwork is filled out. All we do now is wait. It says on the website the school usually calls within five days."

His finger tapped wildly against his leg. He imagined himself on the road, driving a rig. For a long time, he'd expected to bounce around from one dead end job to another until the lights went out.

Those five days crawled.

The call finally came, and he took it eagerly. When they told him he'd been accepted, he pumped his fists in excitement.

During the two weeks leading up to the class, Lester had done as much research as he could online. He'd spent hours on end at the library, reading everything they had. They charged a few cents to print, and he took some of it home. *If only I'd applied this type of energy to school.*

The night before class, Lester couldn't sleep. He'd never been good with others and could only focus on the bad. Fear of his urges came and went, also worries of conflicts that hadn't happened. There were terrible people out there and he himself could be cruel.

The taxi's brakes squealed to a stop. A dirty hand reached over the back seat, expecting cash. He looked at the meter, questioned the legitimacy of the price and paid him anyway. It seemed as if he'd gone the long way on purpose.

Remnants of an old warehouse building served as their school. It wasn't the building they cared about as much as the parking lot. A couple of people stood outside smoking. They were talking back and forth, mentioning how a local mill had gone under and they were out of work.

He kept his head down as he walked past.

Stepping into the classroom, Lester couldn't help feeling an ounce of pride. He hadn't accomplished much in his life, and he planned on seeing this all the way through. If his mother wasn't proud, he'd be proud of himself.

A handful of people sat at desks probably donated from the local high school. An ugly chalkboard stood at the front of the room with a name written on it "Mr. Epstein."

A man with frail gray hair walked to the front of the room. He introduced himself as the teacher and began explaining the basics. He spoke of his years of experience and even told a couple of anecdotes. He'd been working consistently for thirty years in his career, various different types of trucks and loads.

Even the introduction fascinated Lester, who scribbled endless notes, like a kid in his favorite class. Although he'd never been a good student, he planned on breaking that mold.

Some of his classmates didn't share his enthusiasm. As a matter of fact, a couple of them looked like they were falling asleep. Not only had he been fully engaged, but he'd also asked questions.

By the end of the class, he'd successfully taken pages of notes. The teacher had given him a couple of handouts to look over when he got home, but otherwise they hadn't looked at a truck. That part he didn't like. Lester felt as if he were the only one taking the class seriously, which burned him up inside.

A group of men leaned against the wrecked warehouse. Some smoking cigarettes, others talking. They all wanted to know how long the class would take and how fast they could get on the road. They wanted the license but didn't want to do the work. Again, they complained about the mill shutting down.

Out of nowhere the urge came over him.

The taxi pulled to a stop. Lester tossed his belongings into the backseat and sat down. The door had barely closed when the urge grew stronger. Thoughts of killing someone raced through his mind. This time, it wouldn't be like the last. He'd get his own hands dirty.

The cabby asked, "Where would you like to go?"

Lester imagined jamming a knife into the artery in his neck. Blood spewing from the open flesh wound, spraying all over the windshield. The gagging sounds were so real in his imagination.

"Sir?"

He snapped out of it and gave the man his address.

On the ride home Lester alternated between talking to the cabby about truck driving school and deep thoughts of homicide. The urge started small, just as it had with killing Denise. By the time he got to his apartment, it had doubled.

Just let me get through school.

CHAPTER
SEVENTEEN

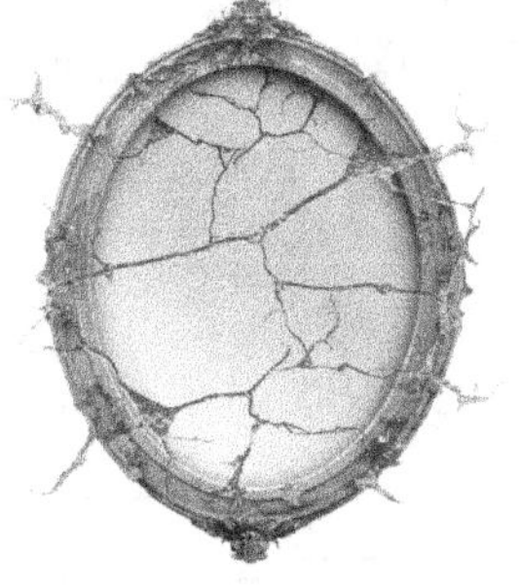

Atlanta, Georgia.

Throughout the flight, Mishka spent little time looking out the window. She didn't do much aside from hold the arm of the chair and resist crying. She struggled to eat the inflight meal, which sat in her stomach like a brick. Every time the plane turned her belly churned.

The plane descended and she thanked God for small miracles.

Mixed emotions swept over her as she walked down a hallway, indistinguishable from the last one. She tried not to think about Anna's weeping face. She didn't want to start crying again and wasn't equipped to deal with her emotions. *I'm never going to see her again.* Then, she pushed the thought out of her mind.

People walked quickly around the airport. She felt small and insignificant until a large, uniformed man kneeled down and spoke to her in another language. One she'd never heard before. She couldn't understand a thing he said, but she nodded. Anna had told her they spoke English in America.

The man spoke a lot. A couple of times she smiled at him, as if responding to his words. Aside from that, she didn't speak to the man who smelled delightfully of popcorn. After he'd wrapped up his speech, they walked through the airport where he fetched her bag from a mechanical contraption.

A man holding a cardboard sign that read "Mishka" approached. He was taller than she'd imagined, younger, too. For a second, she thought about hiding behind the popcorn man, but didn't.

In that bizarre language the two men spoke. The words were much too fast for her to comprehend, even if they'd been in Russian.

When they finished, the popcorn man smiled politely. He gave a little wave before disappearing through a crowd of people.

The man gave her a polite yet shy smile. They made eye contact for the first time. "I'm your Uncle Anton. Anna has told me all about you." He outstretched his hand, which enveloped hers. "I'm your mother's brother."

Twisting her foot on the tile she said, "Nice to meet you."

As they walked through the airport, Mishka stole glances at him. Short hair, tall, great posture. She didn't know much about him, aside from his service. She saw something in his eyes, that same thing she'd seen in Anna's right before they closed the door. Sadness. Pain. Not the type of pain you get when you stub your toe, but a pain that no number of kisses or medicine could cure.

The car door snapped shut. It wasn't a fancy car, not a new one either. The inside of it smelled nice, like new leather. A man on the radio spoke in English, which sounded strange and always too fast to grasp.

Rolling down the window, he said, "I learned English in the military. French, too. I served Mother Russia for a long time before" —he cleared his throat— "the discharge. They offered classes there." The wind whipped through the car. "Oh, another thing... no more cold winters."

Unable to look at him, she stared, slack jawed, out the window. It wasn't anything like Rybinsk, what little she saw of it anyway. They didn't let her out of the orphanage much. "How is it always warm?"

Anton chuffed. "I suppose that'll be a question for your new teachers. Won't it?"

Giant billboards stood overhead, all of them containing one beautiful woman after another. Sometimes they held things, others were laughing together. A couple of them were barely dressed. *I want to be like them,* Mishka thought. *People like them because they're pretty.*

Thousands of questions bounced around in her head, but she didn't think she could ask them all. Grownups didn't like a lot of questions. She settled for one. The only one that mattered. "What happened to my mother?"

Anton avoided looking at her. "We'll talk about that later."

They parked outside of an apartment complex with litter on the lawn. The siding was coming off the building and grass had overgrown.

Inside, she looked around. There were beer bottles scattered on the countertops, as if someone had a party. She didn't think they had. It was a three bedroom apartment, which didn't have much more than old furniture and an outdated TV. Anton hadn't done much decorating or cleaning since moving in. It didn't look like he'd fully unpacked, either.

Walking to the fridge he said, "Sorry, I should have cleaned up. I woke up late." He buried his hand in the icebox and pulled out a cold beer. The top hissed in his giant hand. A puff of smoke escaped the bottle.

The lack of décor bummed her out, but she lied. "It's nice here." Even in the orphanage they had a couple of pictures.

"No, it's not. You don't have to say that." Anton tossed the cap into an overflowing trashcan. "Well, I would give you a tour, but there isn't anything worth seeing."

When she entered the apartment, she noticed an odd smell. The smell of stale beer. Like most bachelors, Anton didn't keep up on the housekeeping. Dishes were piled up on the sideboard and pizza boxes covered the stovetop.

With a beer in hand, Anton led her to a bedroom. There was a bed and a couple of other minor things, nothing special. "Sorry it isn't much," he said.

Mishka stepped into the room and dropped her bags. It wasn't anything like she'd imagined but she was grateful to have a bedroom of her own.

She turned to face him. "What was she like?"

He rubbed the back of his neck. "You're young. You wouldn't understand." His eyes fell to the floor.

Unintentionally, she raised her voice. "I'm young but not stupid."

He turned and walked out. Mishka followed him. When he turned on the television, she stepped in front of it, something the kids in the orphanage had done to her. He tried to watch the TV around her but couldn't.

She hadn't anticipated fighting with him so quickly, but she'd been curious about her mother for a long time. The people at the orphanage weren't lying when they said they didn't know. She'd picked up on that.

Crossing her arms, she said, "Tell me."

A deep sigh crossed his lips. "I'm sorry to be the one to tell you this, kid. Your mother was on drugs. The last time I saw her she didn't look good."

Mishka's arms fell to her sides. She didn't know anything about drugs. "Was she nice?"

Anton set down his beer and locked eyes with her. "She loved you."

Unsettled by the conversation, Mishka wandered back to the bedroom where she threw herself onto the bed and stared at the ceiling. One step closer to learning about her mother and one step closer to learning about herself.

CHAPTER EIGHTEEN

Drexel, Missouri

With a certificate in hand, Mr. Epstein called Lester to the front of the room. They shook and he handed him the paper. There wasn't a big crowd or flashing cameras, but it did feel a bit like a graduation. A small, unenthused clap followed.

He sat back down at his seat, beaming. Aside from graduating high school by the skin of his teeth, it was the biggest thing he'd ever accomplished. One step closer to freedom unlike he'd ever known.

The teacher continued down the list, calling names. Lester had gotten lost staring at his name on the paper. The urge had stopped, if only for a second.

Momentarily he considered calling his mother with the news but decided against it. She'd never supported anything he wanted to do. He had a roommate, Cathy, he could tell but suspected she wouldn't give a flying fuck either.

The following day, Lester spent hours on the phone. He called every trucking company he could find in the phone book. They were all skeptical about hiring someone with no experience. With every rejection, anger and spite grew. A few times he contemplated throwing the phone through the window.

The longer this went on the more useless his diploma felt. All of them wanted drivers with experience, which was ironic because none of them would let him get experience. As his frustration grew, so did the urge to relieve it. He'd managed to keep a lid on it, but it was still there, whispering evil things.

Flashbacks came over him. First, Hercules. Second, the group of girls and sweeping the leg of the chair. Cory. The grinding of the wood-chipper came back with a ferocious sound, filling his imagination and fueling his desire. Denise. Tendrils of blood reaching across the floor for his sneakers.

Before he knew it, he'd gotten to his feet and stormed out.

Cathy called for him. "Where are you going?"

Even if he wanted to respond, that part of him had turned off. He'd become a passenger in his own body, something that had never happened before. His legs were moving but he wasn't entirely sure who was in control. As he walked, racing thoughts came and went. Primal thoughts.

Is this what happens when you suppress the urge too long? Something else takes over. Am I no longer in control or am I in complete denial?

Streetlights hung overhead as he marched through the streets seeing red. All he could think about was the urge. If only he could do it and get it over with, he'd stop thinking about it and move on with his life.

Matthews 6:13 crossed his mind, but it was too late for scripture. Deep down, Lester knew he couldn't stop.

Thumping music caught his attention.

The lights flashed from a nightclub. Pulsing music drew him closer. In front of the club were a group of people smoking. *If there were only one of them and no witnesses.* He fought the desire to look at them because he knew he'd pick one and fixate. Then, he'd do whatever it took.

A trashcan rattled.

He slid down the alley, muffled music reverberated through the brick walls. Lights danced through barred windows above him. When he got to the end, he noticed nobody was there.

A fresh pile of spaghetti sat on top of trash bags gathered in a dumpster. Stray cats and dogs surrounded it, staring with hungry eyes. A couple of them saw the competition and sped off, leaving only two dogs and a single cat.

A Siamese with ribs poking through its fur. It didn't move with the elegance and grace of a cat in pinnacle health. Instead, it moped and dragged. If it were intimidated by the dogs, it didn't show it.

Maybe this will buy me more time.

Hiding in the shadows, Lester watched as the cat closed the distance on the spaghetti. Memories of Hercules came back to him.

It hopped onto the ledge and into the dumpster. Lester pounced, grabbing it by the scruff of the neck. The other animals scattered. It dangled before him. He smiled cruelly at the captured cat, who tried to slash him. A low, steady hiss escaped its lips.

Lester groaned. "Don't worry. It isn't going to hurt ... for long."

The rhythmic music pounded against the walls as Lester spilled out of the alleyway. The crowd had thinned, but there were still stragglers smoking and chatting. If they saw him, they made no mention of it.

Chemical nirvana passed over him. A concoction of feel good hormones raced through his body, like dopamine or serotonin. It was his first hands on experience and what a thrill it was. It didn't fully satisfy his need, not like a human would. He could tell.

As the door closed behind him, Lester locked eyes with his roommate Cathy. A smile hung on the corner of her lips. "You got a phone call, left a message." She brushed down the front of her muumuu dress, clinging to the suspense. "One of them companies wants to talk to you."

CHAPTER
NINETEEN

Mishka pressed her face to the mirror. Her hazy reflection made her smile disappear as she snorted a line of cocaine. The white powder clung to her septum, burning as it entered her nostrils. A few more snorts cleared the residue, and she checked her face.

Harry took the mirror. "What happened with the audition?"

With the back of her hand, she wiped her face. "I try again next time." She shrugged, hanging her painted toes off the edge of the bed.

The razorblade clacked against the glass as Harry chopped his line.

Through the blaring music, she struggled to hear herself think. Just the way she liked it. Uncle Anton didn't agree, but he didn't protest often. When he wasn't passed out on the couch, he was too drunk to care.

Harry ripped the line. "One day, Mish. One day you're going to be on the billboards." He spread his hands in a wide gesture. "People are going to see your face when they enter Atlanta."

She shook her head. "Yeah, right. I'm probably always going sell pictures of my ass on OnlyFans."

Through the cracked bedroom door, Harry pointed at the spare room. "Is that where you do all the filming?"

She nodded. "Anton doesn't know." She waved her hand in a "keep it down" gesture, but Anton couldn't hear them over The Ramones.

Mishka produced videos online. Explicit videos that horny men paid for. Although they didn't talk about it, she suspected Harry subscribed too.

Sitting on the floor with his back against her bed, Harry asked, "Is there a lot of money in it?"

"It's not consistent," she said. "There are times when it pays good. That's why I want a modeling contract, so I can blow this popsicle stand once and for all."

The minimum wage job wasn't bringing in enough to satisfy her dreams of independence. For the first time in her life, she wanted to live without her uncle. She wanted a place of her own, without the scent of stale beer and a sad drunk moping around.

Daydreams of a successful modeling career consumed most of her waking hours. Even while dropping wings into vats of bubbling oil. Selling videos of her naked body wasn't what she considered ideal, but she did get a little thrill out of it. An intoxicating, naughty feeling.

She'd grown into a tall, beautiful girl. The awkward phase had ended around the time she'd grown into her breasts. She jogged, trying her best to maintain a thin waist without developing an eating problem like the other models. The auditions were painful to attend. The other girls looked sickly, but they usually won all the good spots.

It wasn't only her vanity that made her want to model. She'd also familiarized herself with all sorts of brand name clothes, things she couldn't afford. She'd spent thousands of hours watching makeup tutorials online to mimic everything she saw in the magazines. Although her preferred look consisted of mostly black.

The sweet smell of pot filled the air. "Pass it," she said, eager to smoke some. Sometimes the coke came on too strong and she liked to mellow out a bit with her old friend Mary Jane.

Mishka's head hung off the side of the bed next to Harry's. "I'm going to be somebody. I'm going to do something with my life."

Their eyes met. For a second, Mishka considered he might try kissing her. She didn't know what she'd do if he had. It wasn't like she hadn't thought about it, even if he wasn't traditionally handsome. There were a lot of things to call Harry, attractive wasn't one of them. He was kind of dopey in a charming way.

Later that night, after Harry left, Mishka slipped into the spare bedroom. The tripod came out of the closet where she hid it. The cameras were all turned on and they weren't the only thing. When the feed was live, she slid in front of the camera and dropped her black bathrobe, revealing a purple lace set beneath.

Light music played through the room, soft and elegant. Tiptoeing through the bedroom, making eye contact with the lens, she gave them a little shake. The website pinged and gawked with excitement. Tips came rolling through as people spewed their dirty thoughts in the chat.

The briefcase she kept hidden in the closet came out, buckles snapped, and it opened. A series of toys came out. Revealing the most desired one to the camera, she tossed it onto the bed. During these videos she didn't talk much. She liked to leave things to the imagination. Besides, she'd never much cared for the sound of her own voice, especially on film.

As she seductively climbed into bed, she tried not to think about who might be watching. Former classmates had found the site. Undoubtedly a few of the customers from her day job had found her. As much as she wanted to, she didn't think she'd be able to keep her two lives separate.

The purple lingerie fell to the floor, earning more pings as tips rolled in. The vibrator buzzed to life. She laid on the bed and teased the viewers. Things escalated. The music barely covered her moans. She built as much suspense as possible before turning off the camera.

Always leave them wanting more.

She didn't like looking at the chat and only did periodically. Usually, they were married men who'd snuck on for something new. The explicit things they said didn't bring her joy, so she liked playing the mysterious aspect.

The laptop closed.

The tripod slipped back into the closet. She cleaned the toys and locked them away in the briefcase. Before unlocking the door, she slid back into her robe. Stealing a glance through the crack, she made sure the coast was clear before returning to her bedroom.

Lying on her bed, staring up at the ceiling, she thought about her past. She could only remember bits and pieces of her life in Russia. Her uncle didn't do a great job at filling in the gaps either. He told her as little as he could get away with. There'd been a woman named Anna. Her face had been lost to time. Anna had cared for her. There'd been two orphanages and no recollection of the first.

Begrudgingly, Anton told her about her father. The truth had been divvied up over several years, usually when he was too drunk to say no. She'd been the illegitimate child of a Russian mobster named Victor Kerensky. When Mrs. Kerensky found out about the child, her father had her mother killed. The ongoing theory was that he'd had the head woman of the first orphanage killed as well.

The phone rang, disrupting her thoughts.

A familiar grumbling she'd come to know as Harry's fucked-up voice came over the phone. "Mish," he said too loudly. She pulled the phone away from her ear. "Want to go to a party? It could be fun."

It sounds like you've already started.

The comfy bed beckoned her. "I'm not feeling up to it."

Harry's voice became more comprehensible. "C'mon. Do it for me. You know how badass I'd look showing up with you on my arm."

She poked fun at him. "Is it always about your image?" she asked, fighting back a smile.

Harry chuckled. "It is with you, too, darling. That's why you're a model. I probably would be one, too, if I didn't weigh two hundred pounds and look like a troll."

"I was thinking about staying in, maybe doing an extra show. I need the money. If we go out, I'm just going to spend." The thought of doing an extra show seemed burdensome. What she really wanted was to order pizza and watch the Kardashians. Her fingers caressed the sheets. "Come back over. We can watch a horror movie." In a singsong voice, she said, "We can cuddle."

The promise of cuddling didn't mean sex. She'd made that clear. Not that it ever stopped him from trying. She'd always kept Harry at arm's length. Sex would muddle the only real friendship she'd ever had.

Harry's assertive voice came out. "No way. You're going to put on something sexy and we're going to the club."

If Harry ever stood a chance of getting in her pants, the assertive tone was it. When he barked orders at her, or the one time he'd thrown her on the bed ... Chills ran up her arms.

"Fine."

She was about to hang up when his voice returned.

"Wait. What are you wearing?" Harry asked.

Flirtatiously, Mishka said, "Wouldn't you like to know?" Then she hung up.

Rummaging through her closet, Mishka planned on knocking his socks off. She pulled out an outfit, held it in front of her and criticized it. She did this repeatedly until she found something she loved. Her limited funds had only bought her a few great outfits. Gucci, Versace and other top notch clothing companies didn't fit with her Kmart budget.

When she wasn't trying to impress, she usually wore all black. She enjoyed that gothic look, even if her personality didn't always match.

Outside her apartment, the old Buick puttered. It always sounded on its last breath. She hurried to gather her things as Harry came up. When she'd collected everything, she stepped out into the kitchen where Harry and Anton were talking.

Harry's mouth fell open immediately. "Wow! Mish. You look amazing."

Anton sipped his beer and smiled. "Don't get into any trouble. I don't have your bail." At this, he chuckled. He flopped down on the couch and drank.

Her heels clapped as they walked down the hallway. As she passed by the peeling wallpaper, she thought, *I really am a diamond in the rough.* Harry's eyes were on her. She didn't have to look to know. "Roll your tongue up, Harry."

Music rattled the mirrors in that old Buick. It might have been on the verge of dying, but the sound system had plenty of life left to live. Valet parking was a bit too expensive for Harry Dupont, who didn't come from the rich Dupont's. So, he parked it himself in the nosebleed section.

The engine fell quiet. "I think you're going to like this one."

She gave him a look. "I hope so." He had taken her to some awful parties before. She wasn't the out on the town type of girl.

Scrambling to his feet, Harry said, "Let me get that door for you."

As they approached the club, Mishka surveyed the crowd. She didn't want to bump into anyone she knew. Before arriving, Harry swore they were on the list. Just how true that was, she didn't know.

For the second time that night, Harry took charge. He approached the security guard without hesitation. "Harry and Mishka Dupont. We're on the list." When the guard wasn't looking, Harry gave her a goofy look, which made her chuckle.

He put us as his last name, cute.

The large man surfed the list with his fingertip, then looked up surprised. He shrugged his shoulders and lifted the rope. The people waiting weren't impressed. Their grunts of disapproval came loud and clear.

Lights and pulsing music met them at the door. They had to slip through the crowd to get inside. A lady just after the security guard drew a black X on their hands. The dance floor was covered with people grinding and having a good time.

Maybe I can get Harry out there on the floor.

They found an empty booth in the corner. Harry sat down, licked his thumb, and started removing the X. When he finished, all that remained was a little red splotch, barely noticeable in the ever-changing lights.

She whispered to Harry, "I've got to freshen up." Something she'd heard in the movies, but never said before. It beat *"If I don't get to the bathroom I'm going to piss on the floor."*

Mishka made eye contact with a man dancing with a young lady. His hair was sandy brown, and his eyes were blue. The blonde had an hourglass figure. She had a glimmering blue dress that Mishka imagined cost more than her uncle's car. Jealous pangs started, but she fought them off. Eventually, she'd know what it was like to grind against a rich man like that.

I wonder what it's like to be them. The diamond earrings glistened in the lights. The expensive dress whooshed at the hem, blossoming like a flower with every spin. Their hot bodies pressed against each other.

Hot water cascaded over the back of her hand as she rubbed at the ink. She faced herself in the mirror. *Why is it taking so long for my modeling career to take off?* The men online called her beautiful. She didn't have any problems getting a date if she wanted one. *I'm beautiful, aren't I?*

Irritated skin replaced the black X. As she checked herself in the mirror, adjusting the straps on her dress, she kept an eye on the door. She didn't want the staff walking in on her.

Exiting the bathroom, Mishka traced her steps back to the table.

A goofy smile had taken over Harry's face. "Let me buy you a drink."

She slid in the booth across from him. "Thanks."

Harry waltzed across the floor, flailing his arms wildly in mock dance moves. Flailing inflatable lawn ornaments crossed her mind, and she couldn't help chuckling. He looked back at her, almost bumping into a cocktail waitress. He turned around, slightly embarrassed, and walked normally. Mishka doubled over in laughter.

Unable to eavesdrop on peoples conversations, she scanned for him again. The sandy-haired stranger locked eyes with her, causing her heart to skip a couple of beats. Someday, after her career had taken off, she'd land herself a husband like him.

Upon his return, Harry carried a couple of glasses. One of them had an umbrella poking from the top and the other didn't. He slid into the booth, handed her the umbrella drink, and drank heavily from his own.

Sweat lingered on his brow. His finger tapped wildly at the table. The drink disappeared rather quickly. His bloodshot eyes didn't meet hers, which was one of many indications something was wrong.

Putting down her drink she asked, "Is everything alright?"

Harry wasn't a nervous person. It wasn't like him to act like that, not even in a packed club. "Everything is fine," he said, eyes surfing the dance floor.

The same sandy-haired man approached. Harry jumped from his seat, shaking the table. If she hadn't caught her drink, she'd have worn it. Before she could figure out what was going on, Harry and the sandy-haired man were talking. They were too far to hear.

The nervous look returned as they approached. Harry said, "Mishka, I'd like to introduce you to Randall Foster. He's a modeling agent."

Foster extended a well-manicured hand. "Nice to meet you."

It'd been a setup. Harry had gone out of his way to introduce them in an effort to grow her career. *How sweet.* She tried to cling onto that sweet sentiment as the bottom of her stomach dropped out.

Fighting to get out of her seat, Mishka grasped his hand. It wasn't until after she'd let go that concerns of palm sweat crossed her mind.

The eye contact disappeared. Mr. Foster searched the floor, probably for the blonde.

Harry insisted, "She's got what it takes."

Foster's eyes returned to Mishka, assessing if what Harry had said was true. If he liked what he saw, he made no mention. Immediately he looked away, locked eyes with the blonde and waved.

Mishka grabbed Harry's hand. "It was nice to meet you, Mr. Foster. We have to go."

He's not interested in taking me as a client. Hell, he isn't interested in anything but what's between that blonde's legs. As if to confirm this thought, Mr. Foster nodded and walked straight for her.

With a jerk, she turned Harry to face her. "What are you doing?"

He looked down at the floor like a scolded puppy. "Trying to help."

Watching him go came with a feeling of doom. Her career had never been closer. Getting the modeling job through auditions seemed like a million miles away. Sliding her panties into the breast pocket of his suit didn't seem like a great idea either, although she entertained the thought twice.

Humiliation coursed through her veins. Foster and the blonde returned to the floor. Much like a dog, Mishka wanted to tuck her tail and run. He hadn't paid any attention to her, barely even acknowledged her existence.

Disappointment rang through his voice as he slammed down his empty glass. "It's alright, Mish. We'll get you another agent."

Heat rose in her cheeks. "Can we go?"

He paused. Charm replaced defeat. "One dance?"

Harry held out a hand to her, not before wiping it across his pant-leg. She considered rejecting him but wanted to dance from the moment they arrived. *Today is your lucky day, Harry.*

The beat picked up. They got to the center of the floor and Mishka pressed her body against his. She moved with the rhythm, grinding against him. She turned to face Foster and pulled closer to Harry.

The blonde flopped around, losing rhythm, getting sloppy. Mr. Foster's eyes were on Mishka. He watched over her shoulder. Standing under the hot lights, Mishka worked up a sweat and simultaneously gained a fan club. She broke out dance moves reserved for stripper poles. She did everything to win him over.

When the song ended, she pulled away from Harry. A shit-eating grin consumed his face. *Roll your tongue up, Harry.*

Mr. Foster had abandoned the bombshell blonde and crossed the floor.

Not looking in her eyes, Mr. Foster said, "Your dance moves are incredible."

She could have said something to draw his attention away from her cleavage but chose against it.

Mishka glanced at him momentarily, then turned away. "We have to be going now." She ignored him the same way he'd ignored her. She didn't even look back.

"Wait!" Mr. Foster called after her. He ran to catch up. The business card stuck out of his hand, but she turned her head away from it.

To avoid the awkward encounter, Harry took the card, mouthing the words "thank you."

Mishka crossed her arms, looked past Mr. Foster at the bombshell blonde who watched them, full of jealousy. "Perhaps we'll be in touch," she said with a shrug, as if offers were mounting. "What do you say, Mr. Manager?" she asked Harry.

He tried to fight off the surprised look on his face. "I'll have to check the planner." Harry stuffed the card into a pocket inside his blazer. "It was nice to meet you."

As they walked for the door, Mishka stole one last glance at the blonde, who'd sat down at the bar defeated.

CHAPTER TWENTY

Drexel, Missouri.

Wiping sweat from his hands onto his slacks, Lester stared at the meat packing plant. He'd never had a job before, never done an interview either. He couldn't deny his rising nerves. Trucks came and went, moving with precision around the busy lot. At the end of the docks sat a little office.

A clear blue sky was overhead. The building had greenery across the front, making it look nice. Two glass doors awaited him. With a deep sigh, Lester pulled them open.

A woman with big glasses sat behind a giant desk, tapping at a computer. The clatter of her fingers on keys impressed Lester, who couldn't type half as fast. A white coffee mug came into view with the words "Best Damn Receptionist" written on it.

She looked up from the keys. "You must be..." paused for a second. Her eyes scrunched, recalling his name from a great distance. "Lester."

He nodded.

Two plastic chairs, a wooden table and a stack of magazines served as their waiting room. A pot of coffee sat in the corner, and he contemplated grabbing a cup before sitting down.

A man came out another door, dressed like a cattle rancher. Jeans, belt buckle, big hat. He wasn't a tall man, but he did have a commanding presence. Lester wondered if the guy had served as he got to his feet. There was something almost drill sergeant about his posture and stance.

"My name is David," he said in a gruff voice. He stuck out a large, callused hand.

"Lester."

Instead of asking him back to the office, he led him outside. Together they walked out onto the lot.

David moved his way around with experienced ease. He discussed at great length what it took to start the company. How he'd gotten into the business and what it meant to him. As they spoke, the tough exterior dissipated some.

The cowboy walked him through the whole process, covering everything from slaughter to sale. He talked about how much the drivers made and where the jobs took them.

Raising a hand to block the sun, he said, "The job is yours if you want it."

Days passed, and Lester started as quickly as they allowed.

The first trip took him out of state, which was exactly what he wanted. Something about getting away always intrigued him. Escape. Outside of Missouri, people didn't know his history. They didn't know the things he'd done, and he got a chance to be someone else for a little while.

Until the urge returns.

The Texas heat beamed down on his powder blue Freightliner. It wasn't that different from the one he'd learned how to drive in. A country tune banged on the speakers as he drove, thinking about the road ahead. Bliss had come over him in a way he'd never known. Freedom.

What he lacked in experience, he made up for with caution. He didn't want any citations or any unwanted attention. For a while, he played by the book.

Backing into the dock, Lester thought about the dead pigs in the trailer. Refrigerator trucks, running to and from slaughterhouses and manufacturing plants.

A man with a clipboard approached. He looked at it. "Mr. Klass. We will get this truck emptied asap and have you on your way." He waved a yellow gloved hand and the men on the dock started moving.

The truck rocked back and forth as they moved the meat. He liked that part of the job. He didn't have to do anything but stay seated.

While waiting for the trailer to empty, Lester pulled the laptop from his bag. He set it on his lap and scrolled through his emails. There were notifications from one of his favorite sites. One of the girls he'd grown to favor, Russian-doll88, had gone live. He couldn't wait to be parked at the truck stop later to watch.

CHAPTER
TWENTY-ONE

Atlanta, Georgia.

With a loud snort, Harry dragged his face across the mirror. He handed Mishka the rolled up dollar bill and she, too, drew a line. Small chunks of poorly cut cocaine fell from her nostril. It burned. She wished she'd cut it up. As she laid back on her bed, things didn't feel as bad as they had before. She relaxed, falling into the sheets.

Foot tapping erratically, Harry said, "You were amazing." He wiped his nose with his sleeve.

A finger crept to her lips. "Anton is sleeping."

She sat up and rummaged through her belongings, finding the box that held her pot. The nuggets broke in her fingertips before she placed them in the grinder.

In a panic, Harry slapped his pockets. "Do you have the card?"

Mishka lifted it from the nightstand and held it out for him to see. "Relax. It's right here."

Harry grunted, rubbed his nose a few times, and took it. He stared at it, moved it around, then stared at it again as if it were a counterfeit bill. Intrigue filled his face. "Are you going to call him?"

Mishka rubbed her eyes. "I think I'll email him my portfolio."

A broad smile crossed Harry's face. "What do you say we swipe a bottle of champagne to celebrate?"

The smile that crossed her face told him everything he needed to know.

Gripping the doorknob, Harry said, "I'll be back."

Mishka checked her socials while he was gone. There were a few notifications, a couple of new followers and some tips. She didn't bother reading the chat, couldn't handle it, not even high.

Harry returned half an hour later with a bottle of cheap champagne. "What's up with your uncle?" He asked. "I mean, there are no medals or uniform." He handed her the bottle. "I've never seen any pictures or anything."

With the cork between her teeth, Mishka made it pop. "Anton doesn't talk about the military much. Says he left to take me in, but I always figured they kicked him out. He's not all there upstairs." One finger made a circular motion around the temple.

Harry sat down with a bemused look on his face. "Did he see action?"

Tossing the cork on the floor, she said, "Yeah, he was in the Middle East."

The bubbles rose as she tipped back the bottle. On the walls around her were pictures of models and posters of bands. She lay back on the bed, passing the bottle to Harry. My Chemical Romance filled the silence.

"This is it, huh?" He paused. "The key to your future." He turned the card over in his hand, running a finger across the embossed name.

She stared across the sheets at him, clutching the card. "The beginning of *our* future. When I get out of this mess, so do you." She tipped the bottle, taking long drags. Her throat moved with each gulp. "Too bad we don't have any more blow." Mishka ran her long fingers through her black hair and gave Harry a compassionate smile. "You did good tonight."

The night grew late. Harry fell asleep on the edge of her bed. Mishka didn't mind. She didn't want to sleep alone, anyway. She opened her computer for some quick updates. Her mind swam with champagne and cocaine. Marijuana smoke rolled above her with each exhalation. She checked the website and saw donations. Someone had dropped money into her account, which made her smile. She was ready to close her computer when she noticed a message.

She clicked it, and it read:

> I enjoy watching your show. You are very beautiful. I can imagine men throw themselves at you. On their behalf, I'm sorry. You shouldn't be treated like a piece of meat because you are a performer.

As she moved from the website to her email, the message lingered in her mind. It wasn't always a good idea to return contact. People on the internet could be dangerous. She added Foster's information to her contacts and went to the folder where she kept her pictures.

It wasn't until she'd been lying in bed for nearly an hour and the drugs had worn off that she realized she'd sent him the wrong portfolio.

In a panic, Mishka leapt from her bed and ripped open her computer. She checked the sent email and confirmed she'd sent him the other pictures. Instead of the pictures she'd used to get modeling jobs, she'd sent him pictures reserved for her OnlyFans.

Oh no.

Lying in bed, staring at the ceiling, all she could think about was how she'd botched her only chance at modeling. Even if he continued their relationship, things wouldn't be the same. *He's never going to take me seriously now.*

Around four in the morning she got up and checked her email, afraid. While she was up, she went through social media to find him. Instagram, of course. It took a long time and a lot of searching, but she eventually found pictures of him with a woman who shared his last name. A quick google search recovered the fact that he was married, and it wasn't the blonde bombshell.

CHAPTER
TWENTY-TWO

Tucson, Arizona.

The crackle of the CB filled the dark cab. On the edge of his seat, urges ran through his mind. Things he'd never dreamt of doing. The shimmering lights of the truck stop danced on the puddles. A couple of lot lizards smoked beside the building.

He waved to one of them.

His first time, Lester didn't want to appear too desperate. He flirted with her for a little while through the window, gaining her trust first.

She wore too much makeup and spoke with a thick New Jersey accent.

What if it's a cop? The thought persisted, but he didn't want to make himself paranoid. Out of all the transactions that happened in that lot, the odds were slim that it was a sting. Just in case, his eyes surveyed the area, looking for anything abnormal.

Although he'd never been with a woman, he knew what to do. Sex Ed taught him the basics and porn taught him everything else.

The door swung open, and she climbed inside, Lester had to step out of the way to let her in. She moved with experience. Her mascara had run in the corners, which lead him to believe she'd cried recently. The makeup and fake lashes were almost a disguise, but even those didn't work well. He could tell she'd never been traditionally beautiful.

Her eyes searched the interior. "Fifty bucks for everything. Rough stuff and backdoor cost extra."

Having never done it before, he wondered if he'd be able to perform. The thought crossed his mind that it might be chewed bubblegum when he pulled it out. For the time being, it hurt bent in his jeans.

The AC/DC shirt she wore had seen better days. It had a couple of tears and what looked like a bleach spot. There was an ounce of beauty though, something he couldn't quite put his finger on.

The woman cocked a thumb over her shoulder. "Shall we?"

With one hand, Lester guided the curtain open, allowing her into the back. He looked out onto the lot before following her. The jean skirt and AC/DC shirt landed on the floor in a heap. She didn't waste much time.

Nervously, Lester shuffled off his pants. No woman had seen him naked before. He worried she might laugh at him. She looked, saw his body, but made no comment.

I'm not good enough.

The wrapper crinkled in his shaking hand as he removed the condom. He hadn't been prepared for how slimy it was. The wrapper dropped and he rolled it up, just as they'd practiced on the banana all those years ago.

She watched him, unmoved.

When he slid inside, the thoughts persisted. *She's had better.* The look on her face was unchanged, unmoved. The negative thoughts snowballed. *What a loser. You have to pay for sex because no one will do it for free.* She moaned a couple of times, or so he thought. Inadequacy ran rampant in his mind.

As he went, the thought of losing his erection filled his mind, too. Once, he thought it softened. It scared him because he was certain she would torment him if it did. For a brief period, he imagined her mocking him, distracting him from the act.

What do I care what a fucking hooker thinks anyway?

When he finished, Lester pulled the rubber off with an elastic snap that made him laugh. She didn't. Grabbing his jeans, he shuffled through the pockets for his wallet. How comfortable she was with her body intrigued him. She didn't mind being naked, not an ounce of shame.

He handed her the money.

Does she know that was my first time?

Bending over to gather her things, she asked, "Did you have fun?" As she slid the jean skirt on, Lester noticed a little heart tattoo on her thigh.

Sweat trickled from his brow. Not only had it been a workout, but the back of the truck was hot. "It was good," he said, covering himself with the blanket.

Dressing quickly, Lester opened the skirting for her. She stepped down from the truck and started walking away.

What if she tells someone?

The rumble of the engines drowned out her heels clacking on the pavement. She hadn't gotten far before Lester dropped down and closed the door behind him. The mag flashlight hung at his side, unlit.

He called after her. "Hey, wait." He jogged to catch up. "What do you say we get a bite?"

She smiled politely. "You don't have to do that."

He'd never imagined that he'd be asking a hooker out on a date. "What if I give you more money?"

A smile crested her face. If she had any objections, she didn't say.

They walked side-by-side, headed for the end of the trailers. "Hold on. I have to make sure I locked the trailer door."

Looking over his shoulder for witnesses, Lester snapped the lock open, rather than closed. He gave her a faint smile. Curiosity and a hint of impatience crossed her face before she turned to look at the woods.

Smack!

The end of the flashlight dripped with blood. She landed face first in a mud puddle. The mop of hair covered her face so he couldn't see the bubbles of her breath.

Water and mud poured from her hair as he turned her over. Once on her back, he let her go. Again, he looked around, making sure nobody saw them. The trucks did a good job hiding them.

A wet cough escaped her lips, followed by a gasp that knocked Lester back on his heels. His hands scattered through the mud for the dropped flashlight. Her eyes hadn't fully opened, so she didn't see the second hit coming either.

The door swung open. The refrigerated air bit his cheeks. With a handful of hair, Lester dragged her the ten feet to the door. Then he struggled to get her inside. If he'd been able to convince her to get in, he could have saved himself the leg work. He didn't think she would have gotten in willingly.

There were drag marks in the dirt, which he covered with his boots. It took almost fifteen minutes to cover the tracks that looked straight out of a horror movie. It wasn't safe to stay there overnight, not if anyone saw. Checking his surroundings, Lester returned to his rig and fired up the engine.

Cacti and brown dirt covered the landscape as far as he could see. Above shone a brilliant landscape of stars, filled to the brim with constellations. They were beautiful. A quick check of his mirrors confirmed he had that stretch of highway to himself.

The airbrakes hissed.

Cool desert air bristled his hair as he walked the length of the truck, running his fingers across the trailer. He whistled a jaunty tune as he checked the road once more before prying open the trailer doors.

Lying on the hardwood floors, eyes closed, the hooker looked dead. If it wasn't for pressing his fingers to her wrist, he might have thought she'd died from the head injury. Standing over her, he felt that feeling of power he'd once known. That same feeling he'd gotten with Hercules and those teenage girls who'd bullied him.

Thus far the killing had been more exhilarating than the sex.

The hardwood floors inside the trailer were slick. For a second, he considered he might fall before getting her out. With a couple of tries, he managed to hoist her body over his shoulder. She was heavier than she looked.

Dust and dirt kicked up with every shuffle of his boot. Every twenty feet or so, he checked the road. He didn't want to be seen. When he found the right spot, he struck the soil with the spade.

I suppose I always knew this was going to happen. Why else would I have bought a spade? Lester hadn't been that honest with himself in a long time. It felt nice, better than being filled with shame.

Hours of backbreaking labor sent jolts of pain tearing through his muscles. Off in the distance, coyotes howled. He made sure the hole was big enough that nothing would dig her up. If they found her, he'd likely get caught.

Lester pounded the dirt of her shallow grave. His boot scuffed the ground. It looked disturbed and there wasn't much he could do about that. *With any luck, a windstorm will come through.*

Tendrils of pain ran down his back. With the shovel hung over his shoulder, Lester approached the truck. Her body hadn't even gone cold, and he started plotting how to get another one.

CHAPTER TWENTY-THREE

Atlanta, Georgia.

Lying restless in her bed, she glanced at the laptop on her desk. She wanted the money, but she didn't want to do the work. The great thing about her broadcast was that she controlled the hours. In order to perform, she had to feel sexy. She didn't. In pajamas, without makeup, she felt as far from sexy as possible.

Her email exchanges with the agent weighed heavily on her mind. They were one sided, obnoxiously flirtatious in nature and he'd returned a few lude photos of his own.

You really screwed this one up, Mish.

Her Wing Shop uniform lay discarded on the floor. Even looking at it turned up her lip. Once, the vinegar smell had been enticing. Now, it nearly made her gag. She detested working there but saw no other opportunities on the horizon.

Sleep felt miles away, so she did something she didn't often do. She grabbed the laptop, went to her site, and looked at the comments. The same one who'd messaged the other day had posted another. For nearly an hour, she scrolled through the grotesque comments. Although some were half-assed attempts at flattery, they didn't make her feel better. His message stood out. It was the only one that seemed genuine.

I might actually reply to that one.

The laptop lid snapped shut and she curled up into a ball. Before long, she drifted off to sleep.

Thud. Thud. Thud.

Mishka jumped awake.

Left and right, she looked into the darkness, but saw nothing.

Thud. Thud.

It wasn't coming from inside her bedroom, but from somewhere beyond her door. It squealed open. She wanted to call Anton but didn't dare wake him over something so petty.

Splays of light from the fridge cast onto something. As she got closer, she recognized it to be Anton. Stretched out on the floor on his back, foaming at the mouth, eyes rolled into the back of his head. Anton. His body trembled and shook. His foot kicked the fridge door with every twitch.

She raced across the kitchen floor, grabbed his arm, and called to him. "Anton, stay with me! Don't go anywhere! Stay! I'm getting help!"

Pain clenched his face tight. Sweat trickled from his forehead. His eyes were clutched tightly, moving under closed lids.

Stale beer permeated through the small kitchen. Glass covered the floor. As she waited for the paramedics, she clutched tightly to his hand. She prayed, begging God not to take the only family she had.

It wasn't until they arrived that she saw how awful he looked. They'd turned the lights on when they entered, and she saw how pallid and gaunt his face had gotten. How sickly he looked compared to when she'd first arrived.

They carried him out on a stretcher. The shaking had ceased. His eyes were closed.

Wearing her finest black attire, Mishka stood beside the casket as they lowered it into the ground. She and Harry were the only people who showed up. If he'd had any friends, she'd never met them.

Harry took her arm around his. "He was a nice man," he said. "I'm sorry for your loss."

She nodded but said nothing.

Mishka cried. Pressing her face into the crook of Harry's shoulder, she smelled his aftershave. She found comfort and familiarity in that smell, which eased the pain, slightly.

The preacher walked to the funeral director's side. They began talking rather chummy, like two old friends. Mishka turned to walk away before Harry took her hand. She had no urge to fight him off. Usually, she would have been offended by the notion, but now, she felt closer to him. Something deep inside stirred. She didn't fight his advance but embraced it. He looked rather charming in the suit. For a moment, she imagined them as something, an item. She didn't fight off the thought either.

The car door slammed shut. "What do I do now?"

Harry rubbed his nose a few times. "Well, I guess you could sell his stuff and move out."

Fighting back tears, she asked, "And go where, Harry?"

"Live with me."

Mishka rolled her eyes. "You live with your parents."

The engine purred to life. "We can find a place."

On the drive home, Mishka considered it. She didn't want to say no, but she also didn't want to say yes. Living with Harry worried her because he had issues.

The apartment felt empty without Anton. It seemed so much darker. Even with Harry by her side, it was not the same. The living room, his favorite room, wasn't the same without him sitting in front of the TV. A graveyard of empty beer bottles surrounded his spot on the couch. He had gone the way of the drink. She'd gotten the call from the coroner verifying his cause of death.

He'd been trying to drink something away, but Mishka never found out what. She imagined his problems stemmed from the service.

The last month's rent worried her, as did living alone. She'd never lived without him. Even if their relationship wasn't great, she loved and missed him.

Aside from stealing a couple of glances over his shoulder, she'd never seen the inside of his bedroom. He rarely went in there. Normally, he slept on the couch.

Pulling the door open felt wrong, but it had to be done. Eventually, she'd have to clean it and go through his things.

Mishka was surprised at how clean it was. The closet was full, and the floor lacked clutter. There weren't any decorations, which remained consistent throughout the house. Anton's apartment never felt like home.

Harry walked in. "I've never been in here before." His eyes flicked around. "There's nothing here," he said, more to himself than Mishka. A hint of disappointment touched his voice. He finally got into the secret room and found it was empty.

She nodded, feeling the same disappointment.

Anton's belongings dropped into a cardboard box. She stopped every few items, checking them over. Some were insignificant, others were sentimental. When it came to his uniform, Mishka didn't think she could part with it. That went for his bars and ribbons, too. Although they made no sense to her, she knew they had a significance.

Harry must have noticed her struggling because he pulled her into his arms and held her. The tears started streaming. "He may have been a drunk, but he was the only family I had." Although she didn't say it aloud, she couldn't help feeling lonelier than ever.

CHAPTER
TWENTY-FOUR

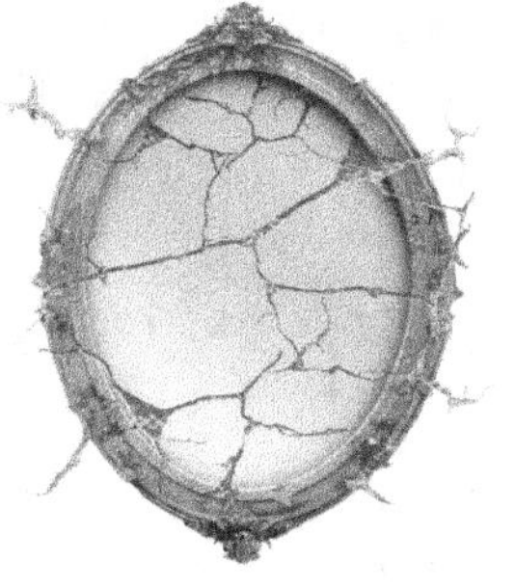

El Paso, Texas.

The roaring engine brought Lester more comfort than anything ever had. Often, he rode with the CB off and the music turned down. At times, he'd listen to Christian music. Although he'd killed a woman, he hadn't completely lost his faith.

In the corner of his eye, the crucifix swung back and forth like a pendulum hung from his rearview mirror. Lester had one thing on his mind, her. He had thought about that cam girl every day since finding her videos. He tried to contact her, but she wasn't replying. Being ignored angered him a great deal.

Lester stopped at a truck stop, clicked on his computer, and shuffled through the website. She hadn't posted any new content. He rewatched his favorite video, taking care of his business. Her account had been inactive for a few days, which made him wonder if she'd given up her sinful lifestyle. He feared he'd never get the chance to meet her. Again, he read her bio. Nineteen-year-old female, Russian descent. Height: five foot, seven inches. Her interests include modeling, music, dancing. Hair color, black. Eye color, brown. Romanticism's include assertive men, tall, handsome, smart, funny.

He sent her a private message.

> LESTER
>
> I hope everything is going well. I wish you'd get back on and post more videos. You're gorgeous and fun to watch.

Aches and pains made it difficult to sleep. Carrying the prostitute's body and digging the hole had been a lot of work. As he lay in bed, he imagined meeting the video girl. He had whole conversations with her in his head, as if he already knew her.

Of course, other thoughts came, too.

During his slumber, Lester dreamt of rapture.

Sweat had soaked through his clothes. His heart clambered in his chest. Hellfire and brimstone had gone through his mind in a torturous loop. It all seemed impossibly real, as if the perspiration had formed from the scorching heat of hell, not the fear caused by the dream.

After half an hour, he settled down. Once he'd calmed his racing mind, he stretched out a hand for his computer.

The laptop plopped on his legs. The Russian girl had responded. She told him she had a death in the family, and she was tending to that. She also told him she'd be back when things were settled.

> LESTER
>
> I hope things are ok. You seem nice. Sorry for your loss, sending my love.

Stepping out of his truck, the scorching Texas sun baked his skin. "Sending my love?" He scoffed. "That's stupid."

He spoke to the man behind the counter, got himself the keys to a shower.

His bag and shaving kit tucked under his arm reminded him of how haggard he'd grown to look. A spasm in his back came and went with every step.

Standing before the mirror, he tugged at his facial hair. "I wasn't much to look at before this beard."

He got to work shaving, spending as little time looking at himself as possible. After that, he spent time standing under the blistering shower.

After packing his gear and stepping out, Lester passed some tired truckers who were searching through the store. A couple of older people wandered the aisles, too, dragged out and tired from the road. At the end of the store was a diner, Lester heard the bustling of dishes and knew the sound well.

As he walked through the parking lot, the urge came over him again. Stronger. More desperate.

Thoughts of the dead hooker came over him, replaying her last few moments in his mind like a film. He hadn't gotten to do all the things he'd set out to do. There wasn't enough time. He was afraid he'd get caught.

"Do it again."

Startled by the voice, Lester checked the back of his truck. He saw nothing unusual. Not an article of clothing or a can out of place. Not even his computer was missing.

"Hello?" he called into the truck to be sure.

Nothing.

His hands trembled as he gripped the wheel. The airbrake let out a violent hiss. Half a mile down the road, he looked over his shoulder again. It seemed as if the voice had been right there, close enough to touch. It had been real, right?

A few days passed and the voice remained silent. Sleep had become increasingly evasive. He wondered if the voice was a figment of his imagination. The further he got from it, the more he questioned its existence. *It could have been someone talking outside the truck or the radio.*

As his insomnia worsened, he started tweaking his logbook. They called it cooking the books. He adjusted the times to make it look like he slept, but he covered a lot more miles than he should have. During his time behind the wheel, he questioned the voice a lot. One of the rambling, tired thoughts he'd come up with was the ghost of the hooker.

Heavy metal poured from the speakers. Cold wind whipped through the window as he chugged down the last few sips of Red Bull, not quite enjoying the chemical taste of it. The can flew out the window into the night.

He tried to remember the last time he'd slept a whole night and couldn't. All the days had blurred together, like one endless road trip. Metallica pounded through the airwaves, barely keeping him awake.

CHAPTER
TWENTY-FIVE

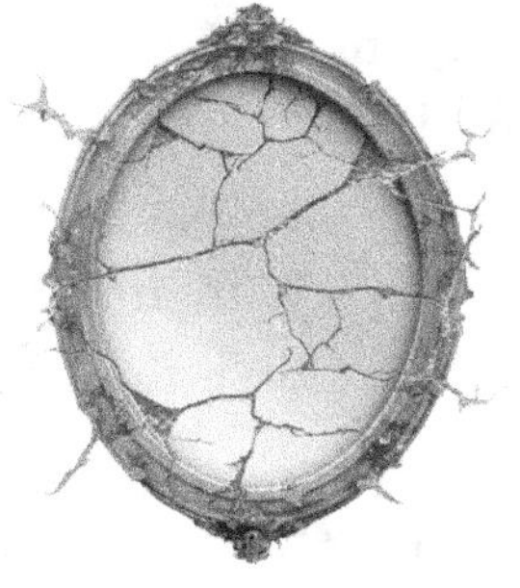

Atlanta, Georgia.

With Anton gone, Mishka searched for an apartment. She didn't want to live with Harry's parents. She always had the feeling his mother didn't like her. Although she'd never tell Harry, she didn't like his mother either. The woman was too smart for her own good. Instead of using her intelligence and broad vocabulary for something useful, she reserved it for witty insults and too many martinis.

As she went through the realtor websites, she balanced a conversation with her new friend Les. A few rentals crossed her screen, which she sneered at. She knew the neighborhood. If those houses didn't have squatters, it would be a miracle. She liked how deceiving the photos could be. She found it comical. They sold it like it was a great place, but she knew better.

The agent probably got mugged after taking the photo.
Her email pinged with a message from him.

Les seemed like a nice man, quick with the compliments. Their email chain had grown, a lot. At first, they were just talking. She grew to enjoy the conversations, and the emails came faster and deeper. Like any flirtatious matter, things began to escalate.

His bland profile left too much to the imagination. Part of her enjoyed the mystery, though. She peeled back the layers, getting to know more about him.

At the tail end of her email, Mishka noticed the time stamp and shot up from her bed. "Shit, I'm late."

The laptop slammed closed, and she ran across the apartment, grabbing her things in a swoop. She'd already been late too many times and she didn't want to get fired. Without any income, she couldn't get another apartment. And she didn't think she could keep living in that one.

Wings hissed as Harry lowered them into the fryer. "How's the apartment hunt going?"

Trying her apron behind her back, she wiped beads of sweat off her forehead. She'd made it by the skin of her teeth. Walking in, she'd gotten the side-eye from the manager.

Smiling down at her phone, Mishka said, "It's alright."

The wings came up from the vat. "You're always welcome to stay with me," he reminded her.

A couple of happy customers took their food and disappeared. She sneaked glances at her phone when the manager wasn't looking.

A hand waved in front of her face. "Earth to Mish."

"What?"

The smile had faded, but his eyes were clear. "What's going on?" He pointed to the phone. "I've never seen you spend that much time on it before."

Telling Harry that she'd been talking to someone would break his heart and she didn't think she could do that. There wasn't any easy way to put him down, either. She didn't know what to do.

Waving him off, she said, "It's nothing."

The search for her apartment continued for two long weeks.

Mishka drove Anton's piece of shit to her new apartment. The interior smelled of fresh paint. She thought it would look better furnished. She liked the white but in the same breath thought there was too much. The emptiness was more than she bargained for, and she considered calling Harry to come and stay for the first night.

She'd inherited all of his things, including his car. There weren't any other family members to fight over it. Driving his car was a change of pace, considering it was a stick. The engine whined a bit and she grinded the gears a few times. There was nobody to teach her how to do it, so she had taken to the Internet. After watching a bunch of videos and stalling several times, she improved.

During the time after Anton's death, Mishka found herself in hardship. She didn't like the direction her life had taken and tried to cope with drugs and alcohol. Harry slipped down a landslide, too. Every day he got worse. She was losing him, and if she didn't create some distance, he'd take her down, too.

The tripod came out of her bag first, followed by the camera. She planned to make Les wait, to build tension. He wanted her, but she wanted him to wait. The conversation had unraveled, revealing more and more of herself. Her real self, not the persona she put on in front of the camera. The only people who knew the true her were Les and Harry.

The email chain had grown long. Les told Mishka he didn't have a lot of friends or family. He called himself a lone wolf, to which she could relate. He told her about the red hair, about how other kids teased him.

She'd been teased, too, so it was another thing she could relate to. She hadn't been popular until after high school, when she'd grown into her figure and out of her awkward stage. She still dressed like a goth and loved her grunge music, but she'd grown up quite a bit since then.

The one bedroom apartment had small wooden floors. The planks ran from the front of the building to the back. The walls were almost all white, like a hospital. The bathroom was the most attractive room in the apartment. It was small, but cute. After decoration, she believed it could be a home.

Without movers or a truck, she'd left her nice bed behind. She'd settled for a futon with hard rails and a thin pad that pushed into her back. She didn't like it, hadn't from the moment she'd laid down on it, but knew it would serve the purpose until she could afford something better.

Her shoes clunked on the floor. She leaned the phone down, facing her leg. One white sock was on, exposing pasty ankles. She snapped a picture of it and sent it to him. She thought it was funny. He found it as a tease. Socks weren't fun, feet were. He tried to convince her to take off the sock. It was something he hadn't seen in the videos. He tried to coax her. Mishka wasn't the least self-conscious about them, trimmed the talons, moisturized occasionally, painted her nails when she had the time.

MISHKA

How do I escape the silence in here?

LES

Turn on the radio.

MISHKA

I don't have one.

LES

TV?

MISHKA

No.

Anton's TV had gone into the yard sale. Some lucky duck had gotten a five hundred dollar TV for fifty bucks. She needed the money to pay for her security deposit. Selling videos of herself online and making minimum wage wasn't enough to hire movers and get a new car.

Light music from her phone whispered through the room as she stepped in front of the camera, hips swaying. A white button up shirt clung tightly to her body, and black underwear peaked below. The blue satin tie hung loose. In rhythm, her body shook. Unwavering eye contact with the camera always pleased her viewers, so it had to work for him, too. Her socks landed on the floor. A bottle of lotion came on screen and the shirt went off. The cream lathered her skin.

Fulfilling his fantasies made her feel sexy. Even better than sexy, they made her feel wanted.

After sending Les the video, she waited for his reply. She didn't understand the foot fetish but didn't mind accommodating. She'd ran into a few of them through her site. What she'd done for Lester for free, she could have charged fifty bucks for.

Compliments and praise came rolling in, bringing forth a pink in her cheeks she hadn't seen in years.

Shortly after that, he sent the picture he promised. Mishka looked him over carefully, observing the contours of his face. He had red hair and high cheekbones. He wasn't the ugliest man in the world. If it hadn't been for the red hair, he would have looked rather average.

Later that night, Mishka felt differently. The hormones had worn off and the flirtatious manner of their conversation had turned into something else.

LES

When are we going to meet?

MISHKA

Well, before that, I have to tell you a few things. Things you should know before this goes any further. I had a very strange childhood…

The conversation explaining her life and the things that lead to her relocation left her feeling vulnerable, more vulnerable than standing naked in front of a camera.

CHAPTER
TWENTY-SIX

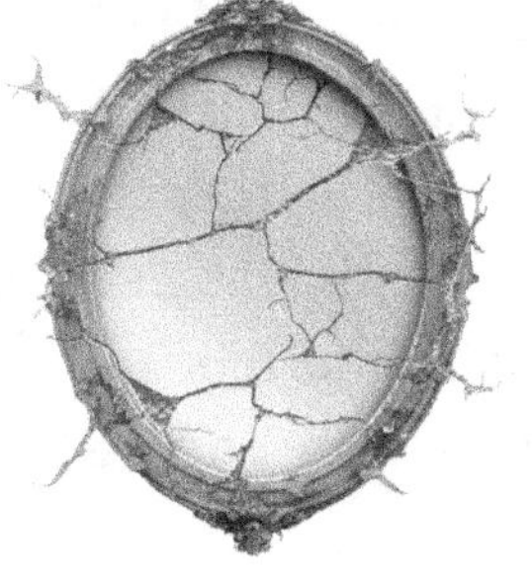

Baton Rouge, Louisiana.

The CB crackled between long runs of truckers ranting. They weren't saying anything important, but Lester kept his ears open anyway. They spoke of cops and convoys from back in the day. Occasionally, they'd warn him about an accident ahead, or the D.O.T., who had it out for truckers like him.

Eighteen wheels headed straight for Georgia. She hadn't specified where in Georgia, but he thought he could coax it out of her. If she'd been telling the truth, Mishka had been lonely and he thought he could help her out.

She'd been eating out of his hands. They were inches away from exchanging phone numbers, which would speed up the process. If he had her number, it would be that much easier to find her. There were apps for that.

Visions of her naked body came and went, coupled with the

memory of sex with the hooker. Those two thoughts played back and forth in a symphony of hormones and desires. His imagination went wild.

The radio promised a hundred and twenty degree weather. Lester had a half-cocked plan to win her over and a much bigger plan when he got her. He wouldn't kill her, no.

You don't kill a goose that lays golden eggs.

All the things she'd told him about her past had brought up a whole new plan, something he wouldn't have thought up in a million years if the circumstances hadn't been perfect.

When the truck came to a stop, the crucifix hanging from his mirror swung. He had a little time to *kill*. The urge hadn't come over him in a long time, but at the thought it came bubbling up. His thoughts, which had been calm and collected, scattered. Bloodlust came over him.

The curved black handle of the CB taunted him. He extended a hand to it. Gooseflesh ran down the length of his arms. "Anybody from around here?" Static hissed at the release of the button.

A voice came back, "Yes, sir."

"What's there to do around here?"

A pause of contemplation. "There's a bar on the edge of town."

Lester thought about it. He didn't drink, but he wouldn't mind seeing some live music. He shook his head. "Anything else?"

With a southern drawl, the man said, "Strip club just off Main Street, if that tickles your pickle."

The thought of dancing women brought a smile across his face. Memories of Mishka dancing in the videos crossed his mind. "What's the location on that?"

"North Bristol Street."

Some of the truckers made crude comments. "Stick a couple in her panties for me." "Motorboat one for me, bud."

He'd forgotten there were people listening in on their conversation and a flash of red crossed his face. The CB went off with a click.

From Main Street, he'd have to find Bristol. From there, he'd find the club.

The small parking lot didn't accommodate his truck easily, even without a trailer.

Even before he stepped out, the reverberating music shook his window. Lights flickered and danced.

One bulky security guard stood at the door, no line. The man looked at his I.D. as a formality before waving him inside.

A half-dressed woman walked around with a tray. On this tray were a few drinks in plastic tubes. They looked like they'd been cooked up in the lab by a mad scientist. Lester couldn't imagine drinking one. When offered, he shook his head.

Another skimpily dressed woman emerged carrying a serving tray. She asked if he wanted anything, but he turned her down. It had been a long time since he drank, and nothing pleasant ever came from it. She tried to sell him beer, but he declined.

The lights dimmed, and everyone's focus went to the main stage. Smoke poured from behind a red curtain, gathering a crowd. He didn't move, only watched from his seat. The music changed, and with it, the vibe did, too. It seemed like the locals became aware they were in a strip club and started hooting and hollering. Lights above flickered.

A woman wearing black lace emerged from behind the curtain. The spotlight captured her. She dangled her body from the pole, sliding around it once. She strutted toward the end of the stage, swooped down to the men in the front row. Her hair nearly whipped them. They went nuts. Dollar bills exploded onto the stage. Men extended hands, hoping for a chance to shove singles in her blouse. The dark-haired mistress stood up, holding a smile before moving away from the crowd.

Fascinated, he found his feet.

Lester approached the stage, trying to get a better look. The star attraction removed the lace, exposing nipple tassels, and she was only a couple of steps away from peeling them off. It wasn't her nude body that drew his attention, but her resemblance to Mishka. They could have been sisters.

He buried his hand in his pocket, removing a handful of singles. When she bent down to take them, they locked eyes. In that moment, he'd decided her fate. She was next.

CHAPTER
TWENTY-SEVEN

Atlanta, Georgia.

Following her, trying to get her attention, Harry said, "Mish, there is something I have to tell you."

She blew him off. "Not now, Harry."

The words he planned on saying would change everything and she knew it. She already knew what he wanted to say but couldn't handle hearing them. Once said, there'd be no turning back. Their friendship would only fall apart because the feeling wasn't mutual.

The wings crackled as she dropped them into the fryer. She did as many of the dishes as she could. Harry followed her, trying to talk. She told him about the new apartment and how far it was, but she hadn't invited him. She didn't have the heart to tell him their friendship was pretty much over. He'd become a sad puppy, clinging to her leg. Mishka had a feeling Harry noticed her pulling away. She guessed he knew there was someone else, too.

The clock punched and she checked over her shoulder, hoping he hadn't seen her.

She narrowly avoided Harry professing his love for her. Hurting him had never been part of the plan. Crossing the parking lot, she could think of nothing else. They had different feelings for each other, and she knew it would have to end.

He was on a dark path and getting worse all the time. Without him, she didn't think she'd do drugs or even drink. Left to her own accord, she'd make better decisions. Her mind wandered to the newspaper on her kitchen table, folded open to the employment section.

When she looked over her shoulder, he was there. She turned to face him. "Harry, don't. Now is not the time."

Desperation lingered in his eyes. "When is the right time?"

She shrugged. The gravel rolled around beneath her feet. A tear lingered in her duct, waiting to fall. She didn't want him to see it. The car door squelched on rusty hinges. She prepared herself for the hardest things she'd ever done.

Misery glinted in his eyes. "I feel like I'm losing you."

"Harry," she said, but stopped.

He ran his hand across the back of his neck. "It feels like you live on Mars now."

Filled with regret and remorse, she fought back against the tear struggling to escape. She couldn't look at him. If she did, she'd lose it. "I have to go."

The engine came to life. Through the rearview, she watched as the only friend she'd ever had shrank. When she was certain he couldn't see, she began bawling loud, hideous sobs. Every part of her wanted to turn around, to beg him to get it together.

As she drove home, she cried, thinking about all the good times they'd had together. She thought about the million adventures they'd been on. She also thought about the drugs and how they'd consumed him. He'd become a shell of his former self.

Sitting around her apartment feeling sorry for herself, Mishka tried to contact Les. He wasn't picking up. Text messages went unread, calls went unanswered. She wondered if he'd fallen asleep. Then, she wondered if he'd fallen asleep behind the wheel.

The thought scared her more than she'd expected.

Remnants of Anton lingered around her apartment. All of his remaining possessions had become hers, including antique beer signs and clothes. What she couldn't sell. His smell lingered in her apartment. His absence was all around her, which made her cry often.

In a last ditch effort at a modeling career, she emailed the agent. She wanted to let him know how she felt. If it meant losing him, she was okay with it. At that moment, it felt as if everything else was falling apart. Losing him would only be rolling out with the tide.

The keys clacked under her manicured nails. "I'm not going to have an affair with you to boost my career. If that's what you want, find some other financially unstable woman." That email took all the strength she had. If she'd stopped to reread it, she wouldn't have sent it.

After sending it, she leaned back on her futon and stared at her screen, thinking about how she'd let all the men in her life down in the same day. She gripped the bridge of her nose and fought back another burst of tears. She'd been halfway through sending an apology email when she received a response.

With trembling hands, she clicked it. The agent had nothing but nice things to say, even emphasizing that she didn't have to sleep with him to improve her career.

Mishka read his email numerous times, speaking the words aloud to make sure she got them right. He did want to represent her. Mishka couldn't allow herself to get excited. She couldn't help feeling like there was a catch. She stared at the computer screen, skeptically. She tried not to get excited, staring at those words.

She emailed back, "What's in it for you?"

"I want to see you succeed and twenty percent."

A million thoughts raced through her head. She didn't know if he was being honest or if he had some hidden motives. Was he going to be present for some of her more risqué shoots? Would he hit on her when they were on a plane, coming back from Miami or some exotic destination? She wondered if he'd "accidentally" book them a single motel room.

The next email made all those questions disappear. "Welcome to the next chapter of your life."

CHAPTER
TWENTY-EIGHT

Baton Rouge, Louisiana.

Heading for his rig, techno music bumped behind him. Even bobtail, he took up a huge part of their parking lot. He checked over his shoulder, glancing at the club and the crowd escaping the noise. It wouldn't be long before they locked the doors. Strippers, bartenders, and security alike were working their way out of the building. Lester climbed behind the wheel of the truck, keys hung from the ignition, but he chose not to start the engine. He waited.

The little red sports car revved to life, lights blazing into the trees. Lester couldn't help noticing the resemblance, even in the dim parking lot. When the car had turned onto the road, he crept behind her. If he got too close, the engine would be a dead giveaway.

He trailed behind her, not close enough to draw attention. He had no plan, hadn't thought it through. All he knew was he wanted her. As she sped down the highway, he pressed the accelerator. A predator closing in on its prey.

A cover of wood unfolded around him. He didn't know how long the woods would cover him, but he didn't imagine long. The truck lurched forward. The little red sports car grew as he closed the distance between them. The massive truck loomed over her.

The bumper crunched as he tapped it.

The car fishtailed; tires squalled. She checked the mirror. His headlights danced in her back window. She also jammed on the accelerator, trying to pull away from him.

Through the back window, he saw her fishing through her purse. He could only imagine it to be one thing. She was grabbing a cellphone.

He couldn't have timed it better, when she picked up the phone, he rammed her again. It must have fallen on the floor because she bent down to get it, almost losing control of the car.

Checking both ways, Lester knew he had time. Using the pit maneuver, he spun her car around. The tires screamed against the asphalt and smoke rolled overhead. For a second, he thought it might flip over.

A ditch brought the little red car to a stop. The airbags deployed.

Lester climbed out of his rig. The sweet scent of coolant lingered in the air. He checked up and down the road. Even though nobody was in sight, they'd made a lot of noise. A quarter mile down the street was a brown house with a two-bay garage. He was certain they heard the tires bark, and probably the crash, too.

Climbing down the incline, he noticed the hissing radiator. A blob of her hair hung from the window. She leaned against the glass. When he opened the door, she spilled out.

Hoisting her over his shoulder, he carried her to the rig where he threw her inside. Several times he checked the road and the house, assuring he didn't have any witnesses.

Once he secured her inside, he fired up the engine. Certainly, people would recognize the sound, but he tried not to think about that. He hoped plenty of trucks passed through. As he disappeared, he thought about the investigation that would follow. He didn't have time to clean up the scene. He hoped that he didn't leave much behind.

Beads of sweat stood on his forehead. His heart thumped in his chest. Sweat slicked his hair and he couldn't stop checking the mirrors. If they heard him, he couldn't tell. If the police were coming, he didn't hear them.

He checked to make sure she hadn't moved. A subtle snore came from the bunk. He'd secured her using a net meant for children. All the company trucks had one, according to Dave, although most of them lived under the bunks, forgotten.

The radio and CB were both off, he didn't want anything to wake her. He also didn't want her to slip into a coma or die. If the head trauma had taken the kill from him, he'd be furious.

Something about the whole endeavor Lester couldn't explain. It wasn't the murder or the sex that gave him the thrill, although those things did have their charm. It was something else, something far more complicated. The secrecy, maybe? The power? The possibility of getting caught. It made the hairs on his neck stand up. It made him feel *alive*.

He reattached the trailer before heading north.

An hour and a half of driving brought him deep into the sticks where nobody would likely cross them. There, he thought it would be safe to change places. Leaving her sitting in the bunk was too much of a risk. If she woke up, she could attack him. The potential of her escaping and identifying him to the authorities crossed his mind.

Climbing out of the rig, Lester pulled her down behind him. He'd gone out the passenger's side, using the truck to hide her body. Once on the ground, he hoisted her over his shoulder and his back sang in agony. *If you're going to keep doing this, you'll need to bulk up.* A protein powder commercial ran through his head, earning a laugh.

Already he could tell the difference. Calluses had grown thick on his hands. The muscles in his arms and back were sore but growing from carrying and digging.

The trailer doors swung open, releasing a gust of cold air. He tossed her limp body up onto the bed and climbed in. From there, he closed the door and dragged her deeper within. She didn't scream or cry. There wasn't a trail of blood behind her unconscious body either, which Lester thought was a good sign.

He got to work, stringing her up like one of the pigs. The chains clinked and clattered as he locked her to the cross bars. He also chained her feet. Still unconscious, her head laid on her chest. Aside from the slight rocking of her body, suspended by chains, she didn't move.

The knife came out of his pocket and snipped open with the click of a button.

He stopped what he was doing, looked closely at her face and still saw a little resemblance to Mishka. Perhaps it was only the dim lighting in both the club and the trailer, or somewhere down the line they were related.

Light reflected off the blade as he moved it back and forth. He pressed it into her throat, considered slitting it and changed his mind. There'd be no fun in that. Instead, he cut the bottom of her shirt, exposing her naval to the freezing cold. He stuffed the cloth in her mouth, followed by a piece of duct tape.

Pointing at her with the knife, he said, "See you soon."

A sharp bang erupted his sleep. Lester climbed out of bed. He looked around outside, seeing no curious travelers. There were no passers-by either. He walked the length of the trailer, whistling along the way. The sun was up. The grass glistened with morning dew, complimenting the smell of the woods.

The padlock popped open, and he groaned climbing in. Tears had soaked her face, accompanied by confusion and anger. She didn't look at him as he approached, which didn't surprise him much.

The air conditioner worked well. Crystals had formed in her hair. A deep cry escaped the rag in her mouth, making a muffled ppphhhh noise. Her nipples protruded from her shirt like candy and Lester longed to bite them.

Chains scratched the metal trailer as she swung back and forth. That sense of power he'd been chasing all his life had come over him again. The same feeling he'd gotten when he maimed Hercules. If only he could bottle that feeling and take it like the pills the doctors forced on him.

He ran his fingers through her hair, smelling her shampoo. Tangles and knots broke with each stroke. She cowered from his hand, stared at the floor, terrified. Tears streamed down her face.

With a firm grip, he grabbed her chin and made her look at him. "You are gorgeous," Lester said, stroking her hair with his other hand. He gave it a little tug. "It's too bad you're a little whore. I wouldn't mind having a gal like you."

Her eyes twitched. The stripper whimpered and kicked, what little she could. Another tear traced her face in a single line. In an effort to scare her, he lapped it off her face. Then he let go of her chin and whispered in her ear, "Don't go anywhere."

That voice returned. *"You should have stuck her like the pig she is."*

CHAPTER
TWENTY-NINE

Atlanta, Georgia.

The camera lens pointed in Mishka's direction, snapping. The hot spotlight made her sweat, threatening to ruin the day's makeup. The photographer moved her with the wave of a hand.

Things were going well, aside from the onslaught of people she hadn't expected. There were all sorts of them running this way and that, calling for him or her. Some of them carried clipboards, others coffee.

When she looked at the audience, she couldn't help feeling like a piece of meat. The few people who were paying attention were lusty-eyed men, her agent included. He'd already seen the goodies, which made it that much worse. She felt underdressed.

If she weren't so nervous, she might have enjoyed herself. Instead, she couldn't help thinking about Foster and the blonde, or the other swinging dicks staring at her, either objectifying her or only seeing dollar signs.

The photographer got up and walked to the other side, camera swinging on his chest. He was a tall man who wore dark sunglasses. He spoke to Foster from the corner of his mouth. She wasn't sure what he was saying but had a feeling it wasn't good. Her biggest fear was that her agent would pull the plug and her career would dry up, a grape in the sun.

A pack of cigarettes came from the photographers tight jeans. When he was out of sight, the other guys busied themselves. Some of them disappeared to set up another backdrop.

Lying on the bed, without any further direction, she felt cheap. It felt as if they'd had a one night stand and he slid out in the middle of the night, instead of taking her to breakfast.

Foster approached, helped her off the bed with a smile. "You have to lighten up, darling. You're all nerves."

The beautiful dress and the amazing setting were nothing short of perfect and she wished she'd been better. "I know. I've just never been in front of people like that."

Foster led her off the set. "Get used to it. There are always people wandering around these shoots. They're big productions, lots of people and money."

The dressing room door closed behind her. Another beautiful outfit awaited, perfect in size and style. This one was a little less revealing than the last. The photographers words lingered in her mind. *Time is a factor.* Mishka tried not to stare at herself in the mirror for too long.

An assistant gave her the eye as she exited the dressing room. Usually, she wouldn't think much of it, but it was the boost she needed. Confidence dripped from her pours as she stepped onto the next set. The stagehands had made themselves scarce. The photographer came back inside.

Foster had vanished. She imagined him standing outside - where the reception wasn't so bad - taking calls from other clients.

Stepping on set, the outfit made more sense. She'd been put in a leotard. A giant box sat on the stage, surrounded by props that read "magic show" which made her smile. The leotard worked perfectly to accentuate her assets.

The photographer noticed the difference immediately.

"Yes! That's it. Whatever your agent said, worked." He came to life, his smile infectious. The bald man with the crazy eyes and tight pants, snapped the shutter like a kid.

She gave her best smile. She'd never heard Foster referred to as her agent before, and it made her chuckle. She felt welcomed by the business. The photographer loosened up. He smiled and moved around the scene. With every snap came a positive reinforcement. Repeatedly, at the top of his voice, "The camera loves you, Mishka." Followed by, "Arch your back a little, babe. Lean to the right."

When the final picture had been taken, he grabbed her hand and shook it. "There is hope for you, yet." An assistant took his camera. As he walked away, he said that he'd need some time for editing but when they were done, he'd email them.

Stepping down from the set, she couldn't help but feeling validated. All the things she'd wanted in her career were coming true. The smile climbed across her face. Before walking to the dressing room, she looked around the set. It looked like something from a movie. She couldn't believe how real it looked.

Foster had left at the worst time. He didn't get to see her come to life. When she got out of the dressing room, she remembered that he'd driven her. That's when she went fishing for her phone. If she couldn't get ahold of him, she'd call herself an Uber or something.

Even Foster leaving in a hurry wasn't going to bring her down. Although, she did think it was messed up. The hot Atlanta sun warmed her back as she stepped outside. That's when an expensive car pulled around, Foster hadn't left.

The window whirred as it rolled down. "I heard things turned around."

"Yeah, they did," she said, pulling the door open.

"That's fantastic," Foster said. "Want to celebrate?" He opened his hand, exposing a bag of cocaine.

She wanted to, with every fiber of her being. She wanted to do it again and again, but she knew things would escalate. Things were getting better, and she didn't want to ruin that.

"No, thanks," she said, turning to the window.

His pupils were already dilated. "All the models do it," he said, waving the bag.

She considered telling him she'd done it before but figured it would be better if she didn't. If he knew she'd already done it, he might have pushed harder. Then, she might have given in.

She thought about Harry, about all the times they'd done it together. There was something painful in that memory. Her heart longed for that friendship, still called up memories of him. She tried to squash them.

Mishka said no, and she meant it.

If the awkward silence bothered Foster, he made no mention of it. He turned the dial on the radio and drove without another word. It wasn't until they were outside her apartment that he turned it down and told her he'd be setting up her next photoshoot.

Inside her apartment, Mishka paced. Too many things had happened, and she was long overdue for a good cry. She missed Harry and Anton. Les hadn't been responding and her modeling career had taken the turn she'd been dreaming of since she was...

The memory of her in Anton's car crossed her mind. The pretty girls on the billboard stared down at her and she wanted to be like them. Pretty girls like that had no problems making friends.

The ping of her phone interrupted the memory.

LES

Hey, sorry I got caught up in something.

MISHKA

How are you?

LES

I'm twenty miles outside of Atlanta.

"I could use a friend right now," she typed. Her finger hovered over the send button. She contemplated deleting it, but eventually hit send.

LES

I just have one more stop to make.

Mishka nervously paced the kitchen floor. A million things raced through her mind. Her fingers ran through her long, dark hair.

The element of mystery surrounding Lester Klass was nothing less than fascinating. She wondered if he was everything she wanted him to be. She built him up so much in her head.

With trembling hands, Mishka gripped her coffee cup. She cleaned the house in a frenzy. He'd show up, sooner rather than later. She raced around the room, trying her best to cover up her mess. An empty closet at the end of the hall caught all the things she didn't put away.

Like from a cheating scene in a movie, Mishka pushed one of her bras into the couch cushions, telling herself she'd remember it after he left.

Les is going to be here soon. I don't want him to think I'm a slob.

The screen on her cellphone lit up, showing a message from Harry. She couldn't handle it and just cleared the notification without reading it. If she were stronger, she'd delete it without reading a single word, but she couldn't do that. They had history together.

CHAPTER THIRTY

Atlanta, Georgia.

The brakes squealed as he came to a stop. He hadn't expected her to text back so soon. Trees loomed on both sides of the rig, which always made him feel a little better. He hadn't gotten into the city, yet. He climbed into the bunk and took a look at his phone.

The girl in the back had to go. He had a date.

Gritting his teeth, Lester pried open the doors. Light raced into the empty, dark, trailer. Footfalls echoed off the walls as he approached. Ice had frozen in clumps throughout her hair. Tears had come and gone possibly hundreds of times. Her eyes were clenched shut.

With the back of his hand, he caressed her cheek. "It's your lucky day. I don't have time to do what I planned."

Her body trembled at his touch.

She wouldn't open her eyes.

Those beautiful feet were only inches away, but he didn't have time to appreciate them. There were a lot of things he didn't have time for. As he considered this, he got to work unchaining her. He couldn't allow her to be free, so he fastened her chain to a carabiner on his belt.

From the hook, he lowered her to the ground. "I know you want to run, but I can't let you do that. I'm going to chain you up in the woods for a few hours. I'll come back for you."

She still hadn't opened her eyes, but she nodded.

The door creaked open, just enough to check if the coast was clear. He didn't like having her on a chain in broad daylight, too risky. When he was certain they were good, he jumped down and hoisted her to the ground. Without a choice, she opened her eyes.

With a push, she sprang for the woods, down the grassy embankment. The chains jangled between them. There wasn't a soul in sight, and he hoped it would remain that way. Awful things would happen if an innocent hiker crossed their path.

Thick trees covered them on all sides. From the woods, Lester couldn't see any cars on the road. He couldn't hear any either.

As they walked, the stripper wept. Light, unpleasant cries.

With a slight tug of the chain, she stopped. The cries got louder. Again, she wasn't looking at him and he couldn't blame her.

A muffled cry escaped the rag. He made out the words, "Kill me." He thought it was part of a sentence too long to be "Don't kill me," so most likely "You don't have to kill me."

He sneered. "Let me guess. You won't tell?"

With one harsh kick, she folded his right knee. A loud pop sounded from beneath his stained jeans. He fell in some tall grass. Obscenities escaped his lips as he fought to regain his feet. The chain broke his belt and pulled away from him in a rattling tail. It didn't take long before it was out of reach.

Finding his feet, Lester realized the knee couldn't bear his weight. More colorful language escaped his lips as he hobbled behind her. The chain slipping further and further away.

That hideous voice came back. *"Get her. Do it, now."*

The consequences of getting caught hadn't set in before her escape. Obvious things had crossed his mind: cops, and jail. There'd be a trial and some half-wit attorney would call him insane, which he probably could make a good case for.

He couldn't get caught, not yet. His work wasn't finished. He'd only just begun his plan for Mishka. It went so much further than just kidnapping. When he was finished...

A bolt of pain shot up the length of his leg and bit into his hip. The dead foot dragged in the dirt as he trailed the girl, losing sight of her more by the second.

When she hit the incline, she slowed down. This gave him a chance to sprint. Each step brought fiery red pain that made him wince. Finally, he caught up. One hard stomp on the chain was all it took. The stripper folded at the waist, let out an *oof* noise, before collapsing and rolling down the hill before him.

Lester leaned down next to her. He didn't dare press his ear to her chest. Instead, he put his hand in front of her nose, making sure she was still breathing. She was still alive, but her breath was rather shallow. She didn't look as attractive as she had on stage. The lust for her had faded. Her hair was a mess, clotted with blood.

The urge to ravage her had fled.

Flinging her over his shoulder had been the worst experience of his life. Agony ran from his knee, pain rippled in his back. A couple of times he dropped her. When he'd gotten her secured to a tree, he went back for the shovel.

Walking back to the truck, he grumbled obscenities under his breath. "Fuckin' bitch. I should rip out her tongue and shove it up her ass."

Digging the hole had been a nuisance, but he finished. A pain ripped through his back, reminding him that killing for a hobby was more than just taxing. His knee also shot waves of pain, which agitated his side. With a couple of pats on top, he finished her shallow grave.

Beside the hole in the ground, Lester collapsed. If not for the pain, he might have blacked out from exhaustion. For a while, he stared up at the blue sky, contemplating a different hobby. He hadn't even gotten the thrill of killing this one.

She was only a test run.

CHAPTER
THIRTY-ONE

Atlanta, Georgia.

Mishka was dressed to kill. Never had she tried so hard to impress a man, not even her agent. She couldn't wait until Les came to the door. Over the hours prior, Mishka had laid some ground rules. For the first two dates, sex was off the table. Yes, he'd seen her naked before, but she wanted to know they had something real before taking it to the next level.

The doorbell rang.

Her hands trembled as she adjusted herself in the mirror. Before opening the door, she took a huge breath.

Upon opening it, she realized he looked exactly like the pictures. Red hair, average face, jeans, and a polo shirt. He cleaned up nice for a trucker. Average looking wasn't so bad, after all. It was what was on the inside that mattered.

Lester extended a hand, which enveloped hers. Hard calluses gently squeezed her fingers. She'd done her nails and makeup and hoped he noticed.

"Nice to finally meet you," Lester said. His eyes surveyed the place.

Remembering how messy it was, she asked, "Do you want to go out for coffee?"

With a pleasant smile, he said, "That would be nice."

The two walked in the hot Atlanta sun. She did most of the talking. As they walked, she stole glances at him and wondered if she were talking too much. Sometimes she got excited and talked too much, some guys didn't like that.

He's a good listener.

Mishka sat down in a booth by the window. She had grown fond of the little pizza joint. It was the only place on her block that served food, and luckily, good food. Lester sat across from her, looking around. Those curious eyes took on the place, like they had her apartment.

Although it wasn't known for its coffee, it turned out to be warm and not too bad. As far as coffee went, if you poured enough sugar in it, it all tasted the same.

Among the good qualities, he had nice teeth. She'd been interested in a couple of guys right after school who had neglected theirs. The haircut looked professionally done, which meant he didn't have any problem grooming. Clean shave, which she preferred. The mountain man look did nothing for Mishka.

For hours they sat in that booth, drinking coffee, getting to know each other. It didn't seem like work, keeping the conversation alive. He still didn't talk as much as her, but she expected that.

With the cup inches from his lips, Lester said, "This is a nice little place you got here. Quaint."

With some of the tension melted, he'd relaxed a little. At times, she even caught him smiling. He had a nice smile, almost child-like. At times he winced in pain, which made her wonder if he'd been injured on the job.

I like him. I hope he plans on coming back to Atlanta, soon.

They'd ordered finger food, fries, and mozzarella sticks. As she ate one of the mozzarella sticks, the cheese pulled really far, which made them both laugh.

"Did I tell you the photoshoot went well? They're going to have me back."

There was something in his eyes unlike anything she'd seen before. Once or twice, she'd caught him looking at her boobs. She expected that, too.

He bit into a fry. "That's fantastic. You certainly have what it takes."

Taking him back to her place would give him the wrong impression. She didn't want to sleep with him, yet. Not that the thought hadn't crossed her mind. Also, her uncle's warning came to mind. He'd warned her about people on the Internet and about how dangerous they could be.

To avoid the awkward moments, Mishka shook his hand. "It was nice to meet you. I hope we can do this again."

He took her hand, brandished a pleasant smile, and planted his lips on the back of it. "I hope we do."

Floating on air, Mishka walked back to her apartment. She couldn't think of anything but him and those beautiful, odd eyes. It wasn't the color, but something unexplainable. She'd grown tired and wanted nothing more than to take a nap on her couch.

Walking down the street had become quite an effort. Yawns came frequently. As she walked up the stairs, she wondered if she might be coming down with something because she felt fatigued. She struggled getting the keys in the door.

Once she laid down, her eyes closed.

CHAPTER THIRTY-TWO

Atlanta, Georgia.

I can't believe she gave me her address. This was a lot easier than I expected.

Creaking the door open, Lester saw her lying on the couch. The drugs had worked perfectly. A handful of sleeping pills he'd crushed and slid into her cup. For the first time since they met, she'd gone quiet. He couldn't help laughing at this as he stepped inside and closed the door. Parking a big rig on the street in a residential neighborhood was enough to draw attention. Luckily, he'd gone bobtail and wasn't planning on staying long.

She hadn't even locked the door behind her. He'd simply walked in off the street, expecting something that would slow him down or deter her capture.

The coffee table slid across the floor and the rug came out from under it easy enough. Her body thudded on the ground, hopefully not loud enough to warrant any attention. Rolling her up proved to be a chore. He searched her apartment far and wide, found what he'd been looking for and stuffed her camera, tripod, and computer into a duffle bag.

With the rug flung over his shoulder, he walked down the hallway. Pain surged through his leg, screaming, and aching with every step. He meant to get it checked out by a doctor. He took his time, hoping none of the residents would come out of their apartment to help. The last thing he needed were witnesses. With his free hand, he carried her equipment.

The stretch between the apartment and his truck proved to be the hardest. He didn't have time to waste. Once they were outside, he rushed. The rug dragged across the pavement, and he had to hoist her up onto the passenger's side. It took all of his strength and his body begged for him to quit.

Lester didn't stop, didn't look around to see if anyone had watched him. He simply hauled ass around the rig and fired up the engine. There were too many things that could go wrong grabbing someone in broad daylight like that, too much risk.

If not for the voice in his head, which had gradually gotten worse, he would have waited. There were easier ways, much easier. Once they were on the road, the voice came to life. *"kill her,"* it said.

"No. That's not part of the plan."

It didn't respond.

Switching from the truckers channel to the police frequency on the CB always helped ease his paranoia. They spoke about a lot of things on that channel, current things. If a mad trucker were to kidnap a young woman, it might come up.

Ten miles of highway took him to the rest area where he'd left his trailer. When he'd successfully hooked them up, he managed to breathe an ounce of relief.

Eighteen wheels strolled down the highway, blending in with all the other trucks there. He continued to listen to the police channel, hoping he wouldn't hear anything. They'd figure it out, eventually. She wouldn't show up to work or someone would come looking for a borrowed book or something. Then, they'd know.

She didn't have a lot of friends, that much he knew for sure. He really only worried about one. Harry. In all the time they'd been talking, she only mentioned him. Aside from her agent, which she talked about infrequently and never in a positive light. When she didn't show up for a shoot, he'd know something was up.

CHAPTER
THIRTY-THREE

Somewhere in Georgia

Mishka's eyes opened to the endless dark. Her head spun as she desperately searched, looking for something, anything. She wasn't in her apartment any longer. Just by the darkness and the smell, she knew that.

As she pressed her memories, she realized they were a bit hazy. After the date, she walked home. There, she began to feel a bit woozy. She wasn't positive but could have sworn she'd fallen asleep on the couch.

The room shook and her first thought was an earthquake. As it shook, she tried to find her feet and couldn't. Chains jangled somewhere in the darkness. Pressure around her ankle led her to believe she'd been captured.

Beyond the walls came the rumble of an engine.

The trailer shook steadily. Every bump met the sound of jumping chains. Her mind was scattered, panicking. She felt like a wild animal in a snare. Panicked thoughts raced around, recalling how some animals chewed off their limbs when stuck.

Streams ran down her chilling face. A mechanical hum sounded from above, like a giant fan. She couldn't see, but it instantly began pouring out frigid air. There were no traces of light, so she guessed it was dark outside.

As the temperature descended, she considered the possibility of freezing to death. It had grown unreasonably cold in a short period of time. The irony of freezing to death in Georgia wasn't lost on her. Just outside the walls it was likely eighty or more degrees. *But we're not in Georgia anymore*, she thought and cringed.

He's a truck driver.

It all came crashing in on her. Her uncle had been right about trusting people on the Internet. More tears ran down her face.

She hadn't worn shorts before, of that much she remembered. On the rare occasions she did wear them, she either swam or tanned. Not only had he taken her, but he'd also changed her clothes, which made her feel even more violated.

Why do I feel drunk?

Mishka couldn't fight off the chemically induced blackout right around the corner. When she awoke again, the truck had stopped. Light speckles came from under the doors, at the end of what seemed like a hundred-foot hallway. It was just a little dot.

Muscles in her neck and back cramped from the cold, hard floors. Pain ripped up and down her side, along with a massive headache. The chain rattled as she rubbed the soreness from her back.

She considered screaming but feared Lester was nearby. Screaming wasn't going to save her, more than likely it would get her killed. She wondered why he hadn't gagged her. She walked as far as the chain would allow, then pressed one ear to the side of the trailer. She listened, trying to hear past the buzzing air conditioner.

A loud clunking noise threatened to break through the door. Mishka stared into the darkness, waiting for the light. She wanted to know for sure who her captor was. The door opened, and the light raced in, flooding around the silhouette of a man. Lester climbed into the back of the truck and walked down the wooden floor. His footsteps fell like dropping lumber. The cold air ran out of the trailer, and for a second Mishka thought she could feel the Georgia sun. The door closed behind him.

"How dare you," Mishka said. "How dare you. You son of a bitch."

He gave her a twisted smile, adjusting the chains. She asked what he was doing, but he remained silent. They dragged across the wooden floor as he set them up in a new fashion. They were attached to hooks on the walls. Once they were ready, Lester hoisted her up. Lying on the floor wasn't an option anymore.

If not for her aching body and foggy mind, she'd have put up more of a fight. "Don't do this."

He ignored her.

When her hands and feet were fastened, he pulled out a rag from his pocket and stuffed it into her mouth. She tried to scream. He kicked her shin in protest.

Her muffled voice came through the rag. "Mphh."

Lester's feet echoed down the trailer, closing the door behind him. The darkness consumed Mishka in a never-ending shadow. Through the fog, she couldn't formulate a plan to escape.

Good work, Mish. You get your dream job, the opportunity of a lifetime and the day after, you get kidnapped by a psychopath trucker. You screwed the pooch on this one. The voice in her head was relentless.

The rag in her mouth had a copper tinge, like blood. The very thought made her want to vomit. Moving her jaw and hands, she tested the limits of both the chain and gag. She didn't have much room, certainly not enough to slip her hand out.

With no access to a clock, Mishka kept no time. Exhausted, she often slept to protect her from the cold. When she was asleep, she wasn't chained. There she was free.

Mishka dreamt of her mother, which never happened before. She found comfort in those hours of absence. Her mother, or what portrayed her mother, was a beautiful, charismatic woman. They stood in a field together, with wildflowers surrounding their ankles. The flowers looked like a rainbow, which stretched as far as her eyes could see.

The truck lurched forward, banging Mishka's head on the wall. Pain shot through her like a hammer to a finger. She tried to scream, but the gag stopped her. With her arms overhead and bound she wasn't getting proper blood flow, which caused her fingers to go numb. Even if they weren't bound, she thought they'd be numb from the cold.

A full bladder caused her a great deal of discomfort.

She fixed her eyes into the darkness. With some effort, she convinced herself to piss. The warm urine ran down her shorts. At first, it felt amazing, warming her legs. She basked in the warmth momentarily but quickly felt ashamed. Droplets trickled on the floor below her. The putrid smell surrounded her.

The engine stopped.

If the truck stopped, he's coming back here.

The latch on the trailer rattled. A noise Mishka grew to despise. Distantly, she thought about the urine dripping from her shorts. Throughout their long conversations she'd never picked up on any red flags. She felt like a fool, falling right into his trap. It made her ill.

With a whimper in her voice, Mishka said, "You're not the wolf, Mish. You're the sheep."

She followed the beam of light with her eyes. It danced on the cavernous walls. He looked scary in the flashlight glow. It showed on her, first at her face and then descended. If he planned on saying something, he didn't. The light shone on the floor, illuminating a bag.

A lantern came from it and landed on the floor with a thump. With the click of a button, the darkness receded. Lester's evil face came from the shadows. He planned on being there for a bit, judging by the sweatshirt he'd worn.

More things came from the bags he'd brought in. Her laptop,

followed by her camera and tripod. A horrible feeling sank in the pit of her stomach. Whatever he planned on filming wasn't good. They weren't about to put on a puppet show for the internet.

A couple of adjustments to the camera put the lens on her. The star of a show she didn't know about and didn't want to participate in. Nausea swept over her, and she thought she might puke.

The gag came out of her mouth with a quick jerk.

Instead of screaming, she sniffled and looked down at the ground. It wasn't the reaction Lester anticipated, so he stomped on her toe. She jerked, lifting her head in a quick jolt. She opened her mouth to scream but fought back. Pain shot through the top of her foot as the muscle spasmed. *It's not numb anymore*, she thought.

In a menacing voice, Lester said, "Go ahead and scream. You know you want to."

Mishka said, "Fuck you." The tension in her jaw made her face hurt.

One smack and blood flung from her mouth, landing on the wall to her left. Her cheek stung. Apart from her pride, she didn't think anything broke. The red light on the camera drew her attention. She couldn't believe he was doing this. He could access the webcam site under her name. She had the password saved, and she imagined that was his plan. He was going to upload the footage directly to the site, enticing her audience to watch.

What kind of sick game is this?

Coppery blood filled the space between teeth and lip.

Before stepping in front of the camera, Lester pulled up his hood. Protecting his identity was still important, apparently. "Say you're sorry."

Her face ached. "I'm sorry," she squealed, pulling away. When her eyes closed, stars danced in her vision. The ache in her face surpassed the pain in her foot. "Don't do this." The tears raced down her face. She couldn't believe this was happening. Her body trembled, not only from the temperature.

She considered calling him by name, telling the audience who he was. She didn't for fear of consequence.

Leaning close, he whispered in her ear, "People are watching. Isn't that what you wanted?"

Back and forth Lester paced, whispering under his breath. She hoped he'd stop filming, inside she begged for it to be over. When he returned, he spat in her face, calling her horrendous names like "slut" "whore" and "harlot."

When he returned, he'd come back with a hand behind his back. There'd been a sound, but she couldn't put her finger on exactly what it had been.

That devilish grin crossed his face. "Go ahead, cry for help. Beg."

In one quick motion hot steel burst through her palm. Mishka screamed. When his hand came back, it was empty. The pain tore through her body. Warm blood trickled down her wrist, elbow, shoulder, staining her white tee shirt. Tears raced down her face. After seconds of agony, she looked up and saw the handle of a meat hook protruding from her skin.

Never having seen that much blood before, she began to feel woozy. The world tunneled. Before she could cry or scream for help, everything went black.

CHAPTER THIRTY-FOUR

Somewhere in South Carolina

All the research had been done, Lester found an email for a secretary to Victor Kerensky. With the footage sent, he sat back in the truck, thinking about the ransom. It would only be a matter of time before the mob boss paid the money and collected the girl. At first, he'd planned on killing her, until she'd foolishly told him about her father.

Dollar bill signs had formed in his eyes. He'd be able to stop trucking, buy a house, and kick back. Hell, if the mood struck him, he could even buy his mother a house. Not that she really deserved one. More or less, he'd buy it to prove he didn't grow up to be a fuckup.

Millions of plans ran back and forth through his mind as he drove along, he had to be one step ahead of the old man. He'd try to pull something. He didn't get to the top of the mob sitting around with his thumb up his ass.

The phone rang. Lester looked down at the number, recognized his bosses name and ignored it. The excuses were thin. He'd been running to his stops late, nearly all of them. Instead of getting the hint, he called again.

"What's taking so long, Lester?"

He bit his tongue. "Sorry, I've been having some technical difficulties out here. Blew a tire and then hit some traffic."

Although he didn't like it, he had to deal with the boss. If not, he'd be put him out on his ass and then he'd have to dispose of Mishka's body in the woods. He was in no position to dig another grave, couldn't even imagine it.

"I needed that delivery there yesterday."

He nodded. "I understand. I'm getting there as quick as I can. You can count on me."

Once off the phone, Lester had the urge to throw it through the windshield and scream. He didn't like having to kiss ass like that, but knew it had to be done.

The urge to piss came over him. If not for the woman in the back, he wouldn't have minded pulling off at a rest stop and just going for it, but he knew there were risks with live cargo. He wasn't driving the right type of truck for carrying live animals. If there were banging going on, they'd know something was wrong.

Mile after mile went by until he found an empty rest stop. It was only a hole in the wall, but he didn't need the Taj Majal to drain the main vein.

Brakes squelched as he put the beast in park. He crossed the parking lot, headed for the pisser. The stalls were filled with the types of witicisms that always made him smile. Phone numbers for girls you could call for a good time. Lester jotted that idea down in his memory. When it came time to do *that* again, he could always call one of those numbers.

Once finished, he washed his hands, avoiding himself in the mirror. Something he did as often as he could. As he walked out of the restroom, he saw a pickup truck sitting in front. A young woman had her feet hung out of the side. A man stood outside, talking to her through the window.

As Lester walked by, the young man bumped his shoulder into him. He turned, looked at the young man and said, "Watch it."

The young man gritted his teeth, looked like he was about to say something. When he opened his mouth, the young woman called to him. "Hunter, don't." That's all she said. That was all it took. He turned his back and marched into the bathroom.

As he headed back toward his truck, Lester chuckled about the name. Hunter. He liked it. If he ever had a kid, which he had no intention of doing, he'd probably name him Hunter. Hopefully, nobody would ever know that *he* was the real hunter.

By now the police have already gone through all of her things.

If they were to trace the phone bill, which he was certain they'd get around to doing, it wouldn't get them anywhere. He'd texted her through a burner phone. The email he went through didn't come back to him, neither did the IP address. They were likely spinning in circles if they were looking for her at all. She didn't have any family.

In all the conversations they'd had, there were two names that came up. Anton and Harry. Anton was dead and from what he could gather, and she and Harry had a fight. If he played his cards right, he could get away clean. Someone might think she ran away.

If only I'd left a letter.

CHAPTER THIRTY-FIVE

Somewhere in South Carolina

The trailer shook, jostling Mishka around. She tried not to think about the injuries she'd recently sustained. *Thank God, he didn't rape me.* It felt strange thinking that, considering she'd planned on having sex with him, eventually. Before...

He'd taken a video, which horrified her. Of all the things he could have done, he took a video of that beating. Why? Certainly, people wouldn't watch – except they would. She knew they would. There were tons of men out there who'd been rejected by pretty girls and wanted to watch one pay. They'd grown resentful.

The pain in her hand soared and sang. At times, she thought she'd collapse. It had gone through her hand, all the way to the other side like in the movies. She'd passed out, probably had gone into shock, but she couldn't tell for sure.

As the engine rumbled, she contemplated escape. It would take a precise plan. She'd have to use every brain cell she had and would need luck. The chains clanked and jangled.

Why does everyone hate me so much? They should have left me in those woods to die.

The stories came and went. She pressed her memory, looking for a friendly face. What little she remembered of Anna wasn't good enough. All she could do was muster an image of a blonde woman who could have come from a commercial for all she knew.

The only person who ever loved me and I can't remember what she looked like.

The engine winded down as the tires touched the rumble strip, ripping vibrations through her body. She feared the worst.

If she hadn't felt like she was going to puke, she might have been hungry. It had been two days since she'd eaten. He hadn't tended to her wounds either, which concerned her deeply. She knew the odds of getting an infection were high.

He doesn't care about me, never did.

The truck crushed gravel as it came to a stop. The airbrakes hissed. Dread filled her from head to toe, for obvious reasons. She hadn't had enough time to recover from the last beating, but she had a feeling that's what was about to happen, again.

The doors clanked and swung open, allowing in a glimpse of sunshine.

Lester's hollow footsteps echoed inside the trailer. The black duffle swung from one hand, a brown paper bag in the other. He dropped the bag on the floor and turned on the flashlight.

Catching a glimpse of the sun made her miss it that much more.

The flashlight burned her eyes, making her wince. "We put on one hell of a show." He shuffled through his things. "There were over a hundred people watching. I expect there will be more once the word gets out."

He didn't wait for her response, only continued unfolding the tripod one leg at a time. This time, he pulled out a mask from the bag. Mishka's heart skipped a beat. She thought he was going to rape her. She tried to talk to him through the gag, swallowing back a scream. Mishka drew in an icy breath through her nose and tried speaking rationally to him through the gag. Tears stood by in the crevices of her eyes. She couldn't hide them, although she wanted to. What she thought were rational words, turned out to be a series of mumbled cries.

He stopped what he was doing, jerked his head up and looked at her from a kneeling position. She spoke again, slowly as if to enunciate. Lester looked baffled. With a merciless jerk, the gag came from her mouth.

Through dry, split lips, she said, "Food, water." His hand was only inches from her mouth, holding the gag. She imagined taking a giant bite out of his fingers. Although morbid, she couldn't resist the thought.

He raised a single finger. "Ah, yes. We do need to feed you before the next big performance, don't we? I think you're going to be a star." Lester chortled as he walked to the duffle bag and dug his hand inside. During his pause, the beam from the flashlight touched the wall, exposing another meat hook.

A chill ran through her.

With the gag out, Mishka figured this would be her chance. "Why don't you kill me if that's what you aim to do? Get it over with." She didn't feel like she could make it through another beating. She didn't think she could go on.

Covered in piss, shaking from the cold, the girl who'd opened up her heart to him was dead. That same, sweet girl who'd gone to the photoshoot and felt alive and beautiful, also dead. Even if she managed to get out, she didn't think she'd ever be the same.

Lester stopped, a deer in headlights look came over him, holding a sandwich and bottled water in his hands. The flashlight hung from his mouth. He spoke around it. "Is that what you think this is about?" He paused, confused. "I don't plan to kill you, Mishka. I want to marry you."

Did he say marry me? This is no way to court a woman. Her tired, delirious mind wandered around their wedding. She imagined herself in a gown with a chain around her ankle. All dressed in his suit, Lester looked handsome but the bulge of a gun in his pocket bothered her.

He fed her, mindful of his fingers. After, he returned the gag.

Once the tripod had been set up, he adjusted the camera. Shortly after that, he pulled down the ski mask. Her heart thundered in her chest. The urge to vomit came over her in waves.

His belt jingled as he took it off.

At first, the whips weren't bad. They were more noise than pain. She'd had worse during kinky sex, but she wouldn't tell him that. After several of these slaps – enough to turn the skin pink – he went harder.

A thick vein stood out on the side of his neck, plump and full of blood. "You will repent for you sins." The vein throbbed as his voice grew louder. "It's not too late to be forgiven, Mishka." She wished she could stick a meat hook through his neck and spill blood all over the floor.

Religion hadn't been a part of their conversations. He'd never mentioned God. All of this struck her as odd, and she wondered if it were some sort of performance for the camera. Something he was doing to increase views.

Through the wet rag, Mishka mumbled a half attempted apology. Lester grabbed her by the hair and pulled the gag out. She looked at the camera, wishing there was another way, unsure what he was doing. She didn't want to cave, not in front of the camera. She wanted the audience to think she was strong, clinging to the only thing she had left, pride.

The slap across her face stung. "Again!" he shouted.

Her eyes danced around in her head, making splotches in her vision. Shaking her head didn't clear it. Bright colors fizzled in her periphery like a kaleidoscope.

The ski mask didn't make it scarier. If anything, it made the process easier because then she didn't have to think about his betrayal. All she could see on his face were those eyes. The eyes of a tortured animal.

Careful to stay out of the view of the lens, Lester walked around her. The belt patted against the legs of his jeans. That's when she came up with an idea. There wouldn't be any more videos if he didn't have an audience. She just had to break the camera.

Lester cocked back his giant fist, smashing his knuckles into her rib cage. A bolt of pain shot down her side. Waves of unspeakable agony swept over her. Something felt broken. With the gag in hand, he walked toward her.

Before he could silence her, she spoke. "Don't you want to get a close-up, sick fuck? Make sure the audience sees that I'm not faking it."

He turned his head in response. All the while he was thinking, Mishka made sure her leg would have enough swing to hit him, or the camera, whichever got closest. He grabbed the tripod, stepping forward to take the shot, instilling horror in the viewers. The eight-foot gap closed into barely three. At full stretch, her foot could touch the tripod. Mishka waited until the timing was right.

With every breath, it felt like broken glass in her lungs. She winced at the pain, enduring a few more slaps. They weren't hard. He'd probably done them for the audience.

Another obnoxious, unexpected scream came out. "Repent."
It startled her.
Once he'd crossed in front of her, right where she wanted him, she swung. Her leg clipped him in the hip, pushing him backward into the tripod and forcing them both to fall over. He shuffled, getting to his feet, and looking down at the equipment.

CHAPTER
THIRTY-SIX

Somewhere in South Carolina

Phone calls from his boss persisted, he'd run out of excuses. He had to do something. If he didn't act, he'd get fired. Then, he'd have nowhere to put her. He couldn't imagine placing her in his tiny apartment with that nosey bitch of a roommate.

On his most recent phone call with the boss, he told him they'd be wheels up in a matter of days. That seemed to work. He got off Lester's ass for a bit. That's when he'd come up with the plan of putting her under the bunk. As long as she didn't kick out the storage compartment door, things would be fine.

"You could kill her, you know," the voice said, assuring him it would be the simplest way.

"I could," he agreed aloud. "That would take away from the longer plan. If I can get her father to cough up some dough to save her life, that would be better."

"He doesn't want her," the voice hissed.

The video he'd sent to the secretary didn't do much. Part of him expected that her father would step in, be the hero and save the day. He even imagined getting a response immediately but didn't. That angered him. How are you supposed to take someone for ransom if they aren't willing to pay to get her back?

By now, the police have found the videos. They know about the site, and they are watching.

Time felt unusually thin. Options were running out. He certainly couldn't keep her in the back of the truck forever. If only he'd thought it through a bit longer. Thoughts of renting a cabin and sticking her there came and went. All the options had serious holes in them. If he left her tied up in a cabin, she'd starve to death, or worse, escape.

There'd been an uncle, that might have worked if he'd still been alive. If her and the best friend hadn't fallen apart, he might have sent the video to him. *Well, I still might.* What little he knew about the best friend was enough to assure that he didn't have anywhere near enough money to be worth the ransom. He also considered sending it to the agent but changed his mind. At the sight of problems, the guy would cut his losses and run.

Lester had bet too much on the mobster's ego.

The engine rumbled as he furthered down the road, headed to his next pickup. He had lost time to make up for, and lying to the boss was growing tiresome.

One of the many preachers came over the A.M. waves. Lester listened patiently, remembering the time he'd spent in the psyche facility and the man in the room next door. Max had done his bidding, only when he thought the voice belonged to God.

He wondered if he could find another assistant. Someone who would follow him blindly, helping him whenever needed. As he thought about the reasons he'd done some of his awful deeds, he figured they wouldn't follow for long. If they did, he wouldn't have a partner in crime but more like a small cult.

"Do you want to spend eternity in hell?" the voice on the radio asked, pulling him from his deep thought. "If so, keep doing what you're doing right now."

Lester perked up, as if the voice had spoken to him.

The radio preacher continued. "Isaiah 55:7 says Let the wicked forsake their ways and the unrighteous man his thoughts: and let return unto the lord, and he will have mercy upon him."

A moment of self-reflection came. It didn't last long before the other voice broke his train of thought and told him to shut it off because they had work to do.

He didn't shut it off but continued to listen to the sermon. That angered the other voice.

The phone rang.

Grateful for a distraction, Lester answered. It didn't matter who it was, he was thankful to anyone who wasn't inside his head, that wanted to talk to him. It could have been a telemarketer, and he would have listened to their entire speech.

The phone crackled through the speakers. "Lester, it's your mother."

Part of him wanted to groan, but he didn't. Her voice had stopped the other one. The call had stopped the preacher, and he was thankful they were both out of his head, momentarily.

"Yes, Mom?"

"I was just thinking about you and how long it's been since we spoke. I should have handled this differently. I was hoping the next time you were in the area you'd stop by and see us. We miss you like crazy."

Lester rubbed the scruff on his face, imagining sitting down at the dinner table with his parents.

"I know your father isn't a man of many words, but he misses you."

Lester gritted his teeth. "Uh, huh."

She continued. "We hope you're making friends out there on the road. I bet it's very lonely."

Lonely. A concept he'd never understood. People had always been more of a nuisance to him than a comfort. Thinking back, Lester wondered if he'd ever felt lonely before. Even when he'd gone away to camp and hadn't seen his parents for two weeks, he didn't remember feeling anything other than drowsy from the medication.

Lying he said, "I talk to people on the CB sometimes."

"That's nice."

The roadblock their conversations always hit came. They didn't have anything else to talk about because she, like everyone in his life, was a stranger. He'd never made the effort to know her, the real her. If she had any hobbies, Lester didn't know about them. What she'd planned to do with her life was as much of a mystery to him as space or the bottom of the ocean.

It wasn't comfortable silence either.

"I suppose your father is expecting dinner soon."

Again, Lester imagined sitting at the table with them, getting those looks. They were unsettling looks, curious and scared looks. They wanted to know what he'd been up to but didn't dare ask because they were afraid of the truth.

"Well, I love you, Lester."

"You too, Mom."

Click.

CHAPTER THIRTY-SEVEN

Somewhere in South Carolina

A *body can only take so much damage*, Mishka thought. *How much more of this can I go through before I collapse or die?* It didn't make sense why he tortured her. She'd been good to him. That's when her mind wandered into uncharted territory. Her body could take more damage and it could go on for a lot longer because there were people who did it for a living. People who hit each other in rings for entertainment purposes. Harry used to watch boxing.

Even if she were unchained and allowed to defend herself, she couldn't win against him. Aside from a few school tussles, she'd never been physical. Apart from jogging, she'd never worked out.

It's ironic, isn't it? I wouldn't hurt a fly but there have been people trying to kill me since birth.

Under ordinary circumstances, she wouldn't hurt a fly. Under these ones, she knew better. There wouldn't be a knight in shining armor who'd come to her rescue. No. She wasn't a damsel in distress like in the story books. She'd have to save herself.

Kicking over the camera had bought her time, but she knew what she had to do.

Above her the meat hook had been forgotten. With some skill, she could wrap the chain around it. Then, she could get to work. It was too dark. She didn't know how long it would take, but if she rubbed them together long enough, the metal would thin. Eventually, there would be some wear.

With the chain pressed against the meat hook, Mishka rocked it back and forth. It made an awful scratching sound. As she did this, she thought about all the things she'd do if she got out. First, she'd find Harry and apologize. He didn't deserve being abandoned like that. He too had a difficult upbringing and probably needed her support, not neglect.

He was after all, the only friend she'd ever had.

For what felt like hours, Mishka worked to grind the chain, hoping it would work. Praying.

Although she didn't like violence, she knew what was coming. There were things she'd have to do to escape, unthinkable things. Steeling her mind for the war ahead, Mishka also worked her muscles.

I should have taken those kickboxing classes.

All the things she'd taken for granted came to mind. She had access to unlimited hot wings at her job, to which she'd sneered at toward the end. The scent of vinegar had made her nauseous. Now, looking back, she wished she could have all of those wings.

Her stomach growled.

The problem with working out was that she burned calories she didn't have. In order to get more food, she'd have to be creative. She would have to devise a plan that would get her out of it.

As she progressed through the hunger, she tried to think about the other things in her life that had gone wrong. No longer did she think she could live in fear of a father she never knew. If he planned on killing her, he'd have to do it.

During this time, she wondered if her father hadn't put Les up to it. If he wasn't part of a bigger conspiracy to take her to him. It didn't seem likely. She just had the worst luck imaginable.

When she regained her freedom, she planned on going all in on her modeling career. She wanted to be on billboards in Atlanta. When people came from all around the world, she wanted to be the first face they saw coming into the city. It didn't much matter what product she had to hock. Hell, she'd have gone for adult diapers if it got her that spot.

Those beautiful women she'd seen on those billboards all those years ago had made an everlasting impression on her. They'd made her feel welcome, hopeful. They'd given her a piece of mind when the rest of the world seemed so uncertain. That's what she wanted.

CHAPTER
THIRTY-EIGHT

Somewhere in South Carolina

The alarm clock rang, waking Lester from a dreamless sleep. As he got out of the bunk, he looked around. A subtle scratching noise came from behind him. Confused, he looked around, expecting a mouse or a rodent to be chewing its way through the wood. When he didn't find anything, he groaned.

Fifteen miles away a slaughterhouse waited.

Coming to life, grabbing his cellphone, he yawned. An email.

As quick as he could open the app, he did. What he found was a response from the receptionist at the desk of Mr. Victor Kerensky. It read, Release the girl.

At this, Lester scoffed. He didn't need a cup of coffee because the anger woke him.

Lester replied. Clearly you don't understand the severity of the situation. Either pay up, or she dies.

He got to his feet and started dressing. The stench of the hookers shampoo had finally come out of his pillow, thankfully. The remnants of the broken camera lay on the passenger's seat, where he'd tossed it, after he'd broken it further in a fit of rage.

Walking down the length of the trailer, he checked for any onlookers. By now, they knew she was missing, and they'd probably seen the videos. It was just a matter of time before they came looking.

I have to speed this up.

The door creaked open, letting in light. At the end, Mishka stared back at him with a disgruntled look. It slammed closed behind him.

His footfalls echoed through the trailer. As he closed the distance, he pulled the phone from his pocket. The battery flashed warnings. He hadn't charged it overnight like normal. He'd been pretty angry about the camera and hadn't been thinking straight.

"Kill her," the voice said.

With a beep, the camera started rolling. "This is what happens when you don't pay," he shouted.

With his free hand, Lester grabbed a knot of her hair. She screamed. He slammed her head against the trailer wall. The chains jangled. Again, he smashed her head.

"You clearly misunderstand me. Pay up."

When he let her go, blood trickled through his fingertips. If not for the snoring, he might have thought she was dead. She'd fallen unconscious, which only made him angrier.

He almost turned the camera on himself. Almost. He'd been so angry he hadn't been thinking straight. If they knew what he looked like, then it would be that much easier for them to find him. A video of his face going viral was the last thing he wanted.

As he stepped back, he got a look at her. What little of it he saw in the glimmering flashlight. Part of him was sickened by what he saw. She didn't look well. That once beautiful face had become gaunt. No longer was she the happy, interesting woman who'd sat across from him at the pizza place. Only a shell of her remained.

The coffee cup shook in his hand as he sat at the counter of the diner. Anger surged through his veins. Breakfast sat on a plate before him, untouched. Even if he could eat, he didn't think he would. It looked terrible.

More than anything, Lester wanted to go back into the trailer and kill her. If for nothing else than to stop that persistent voice in his head. He imagined it, allowing himself the fantasy of not stopping. Over and over, he smashed her head against the wall, blood pouring out of her cracked skull.

"It's not too late," the voice whispered. *"It's been a long time since we killed."*

As the waitress walked by with the coffee pot, he imagined what it would be like to break it over her head and strangle her with his bare hands.

Steadily his foot tapped against the tile floor.

The waitress asked, "Refill?"

It startled him. He'd been staring at her and hadn't even noticed that she'd turned in his direction, or that she'd been standing in front of him for twenty or so seconds.

He shook his head.

If he'd spoken to her, he wouldn't be sure what he'd say. It seemed possible that he might have started grooming her, finding a way to get her alone. He could flirt. She was a bit older, but probably still open to a strange encounter in a dark closet. He could slash her tire and wait.

Before he could formulate a plan to kill her, he slapped money on the counter and walked out. The food remained untouched.

Crossing the parking lot toward the truck, the noise persisted. Grinding. He paused, staring at the trailer, trying to determine what might be causing it. Inching closer, he pressed his ear to the cold metal and heard it get louder.

It's coming from inside. What is she doing in there?

In the parking lot of a busy diner wasn't the right place to swing open that door. Too many risks. Whatever it was she was up to, it would have to wait. Once he'd found some privacy, then he could see what she'd been doing. Also, he planned on moving her into the bunk.

CHAPTER
THIRTY-NINE

Somewhere in South Carolina

Waking up with a splitting headache, Mishka struggled to piece it together. Everything was a bit foggy. Her vision had gone blurry, and the world swayed. He'd been inside, of that she'd been certain. How long ago, she couldn't say for sure.

The chains weren't giving. She'd been grinding them on and off for days, but they hadn't given an inch. Doubt replaced hope as she hung her head in shame. There weren't a lot of options left. She didn't know how much time she had, either. Eventually he'd get tired of beating her or it would go too far, and she'd be dead.

Leave it to me, the first real boyfriend I ever get and he's abusive.

All she could do was stare out into the darkness and wait. Everything within her control consisted of grinding the chains and listening to the world outside. If she had to guess, she'd say they stopped off at a rest stop because it was quiet, not like the truck stops where engines rumbled all around.

After half an hour of waiting, the truck started up and they were on the road again. She'd come to enjoy the subtle rocking of the road. If not for the hanging position and the clanking of chains, it might have been peaceful.

They weren't on the road for long before the brakes squelched, warning her. If she'd made more progress on the chains, she might have tried something. Without even a chink in the links, she couldn't do much of anything.

The pain in her head made everything difficult to process. She couldn't think straight. All of her thoughts were too slow, not like they'd been before. Tears stung as they escaped. *What if this headache never goes away? What if he doesn't stop?*

Several minutes of suspense passed as she stared down the long, dark trailer. He'd come. She knew he would.

When the door swung open, she stole glances above where the chain had rubbed against the meat hook. If only the trailer had been shorter, she might have seen better. If the chains were a bit longer, she could probably grab the hook.

With every footfall, her heart escalated. She wanted to be anywhere else. As he got closer, she winced. The muscles in her back and shoulders tightened as he drew closer and closer. When he finally got in her face, she didn't want to open her eyes.

If not for the gag in her mouth, she might have said something. There wasn't enough time. He didn't say a word, only placed a soaking wet rag over her mouth and nose. Protesting did nothing. She tried to scream but couldn't. Before drifting off into the deepest sleep of her life, she thought he'd suffocated her.

When she returned to consciousness, something had changed. Her mouth and nose burned. No longer was she suspended from the ceiling like she'd been in the trailer. Now, she found herself lying on her side.

Still, darkness surrounded her. In the trailer she had a lot of room. Not anymore.

Voices surrounded her. Banging and beeping came from outside. It wasn't the same muffled sound from the trailer. No, this was cleaner and closer.

A sliver of light came from above her head, long and straight. *What could this be?* Unable to move her hands, Mishka pushed on the wood above with her knee. It moved. Again, she pushed harder. The wood moved again, revealing light and more of the interior.

It's the inside of his truck.

The trailer shook back and forth, startling her to the point where she dropped the bunk, and it clapped shut. Her heart nearly stopped, expecting Lester to rip it open and slap her across the face. In stunned silence, she waited. After a couple of minutes, she decided he wasn't there.

Still groggy from the drugs, Mishka hoisted the bunk up and looked around. With her hands tied, she couldn't do much. Getting to her knees proved to be an incredible feature. It had been a long time since she'd seen the sun, and she couldn't wait to get out.

Climbing out of the bunk proved to be difficult, but she managed, remembering how limber she'd been as a child. When hiding from the other kids in the orphanage, she'd gotten creative. Even in Atlanta, they'd forced her into many lockers in elementary school.

In order to keep the bunk from snapping shut, she stuck her foot in its path. When it bashed against her toes, she regretted it. Pain ripped through her foot and if it had not been for the gag in her mouth, she'd have screamed.

The interior of the truck was meticulously clean. Everything looked in order and in place. She didn't know him to be that way, but he hadn't told her everything. He hadn't told her that he'd planned on kidnapping her and stashing her in the back of his truck either.

Freedom is right on the other side of that door.

Closing in on it, she heard him talking. He wasn't far. Peeking her head out into the cab, she saw Les standing by the side of the rig talking to a couple of guys. They were less than ten feet away. He turned his head, which stopped her heart.

Did he see me?He's going to make me pay for that.

Without the use of her hand, she didn't know how she'd open the door. Time was running out. She could tell by how the men were talking that they wouldn't be at it much longer. Her whole body trembled as she contemplated her escape.

Her cries for help were nothing more than a whimper behind a wet rag. That's when she had a brilliant idea. She'd lean on the horn. Certainly, someone would hear her distress and then come looking. She turned to lay against the steering wheel when the door clicked open.

They made uncomfortable eye contact.

He turned to look at the men, waved and said, "You have a good night now."

In two steps, he'd gotten into the rig. She didn't have time to back away from him before he'd taken her hair into his hands and jerked her to the floor. The curtain that separated the cab from the sleeper ripped shut.

She collapsed, screaming, and crying. Before she could gather her thoughts, his weight fell upon her.

"What the hell do you think you're doing?"

His knees pressed into her ribs.

When he pulled her to her feet, she breathed a sigh of relief. He hadn't hit her, which came as a shock. She'd expected the worst beating of her life, even worse than smashing her head off the wall until she'd gone unconscious.

Pushing her onto the bed, he said, "Good news. Your daddy is coming to get you."

CHAPTER
FORTY

Orangeburg, South Carolina.

T he email had come through only minutes before he caught her trying to escape. Apparently, he hadn't used enough chloroform to keep her subdued throughout. When he saw her standing there between the seats, he had to refrain from beating her to death. That's what the voice in his head said to do and he almost listened.

Mishka resisted quite a bit, but he managed to smother her again. When she'd gone unconscious, he tied her legs as well and tossed her back under the bunk.

Even with the voice in his head telling him that everything could go wrong, he didn't care. He had gotten the email confirming that Kerensky would pay three million dollars for his daughter. As he drove, he couldn't fight off the smile edging the corner of his mouth.

Don't celebrate until the money is in the account.

The preacher on the radio carried on about forgiveness. The voice in his head subsided, after being ignored for a long time. Lester wondered what he'd do to kill three days. He had his delivery and told Kerensky they'd be making the trade in South Carolina about thirty miles from the superstore that bought the meat.

As the miles passed, he couldn't stop thinking about the things he could do with the money. He couldn't help himself. The possibilities were endless. One thing was certain, he wasn't going to live with that nosey woman Cathy for a moment longer than he needed to. There were ways he could make it look legit. Although he didn't know much about laundering money, there were a few things he could think of that would help ward off the IRS.

Eighteen wheels thundered down the highway as they approached the rest stop where they agreed to meet. Although he'd never admit it, Lester felt something he hadn't felt in a very long time: nervous.

When he pulled the rig to a complete stop, he searched around the premises, hoping to see the mobster first. He wanted desperately to feel in control.

Cars whizzed by on the highway, some of them moving much faster than the posted speed limit. There were a few sporadic cars about the parking lot, but none of them looked like they belonged to a man with as much money as Mishka's father. As he waited, his foot tapped rhythmically on the floormat below. His eyes flickered back and forth, hoping to catch a glimpse of him and his goons before they knew he was there.

Lester wished he'd come up with a better plan because he had a giant rig and nowhere to hide it. Sweat trickled down his forehead both from the heat and the nerves.

A Mercedes pulled in. He watched suspiciously as the car drove around the parking lot and then approached him. It stopped beside his truck.

A man in a suit climbed out and opened one of the rear doors, releasing another man in a suit. The second man carried a briefcase.

Descending from the truck, Lester wished he'd met them in a

better place. He didn't like being out in the open. If they wanted to do something, it could end badly. He also wished he'd come up with a gun or something.

The man presumed to be the bodyguard approached first. He barked orders for Lester to stand where he was and allow himself to be frisked. Although he didn't like it, he did as he was told. He would have rather they not known that he was unarmed.

The man with the weasel face spoke softly. "You have my daughter. I'd greatly appreciate if you gave her to me." He said this through gritted teeth, as if he held back a great rage.

Lester nodded. "Money first."

The man held out the briefcase.

That greedy feeling came over Lester again, as he considered all he could do with the money. He took it and wandered toward the back of the truck where he pried the doors open.

The mobster blocked his eyes from the sun and peered into the back of the trailer. Once satisfied, he nodded at his bodyguard, who drew his weapon and shot Lester Klass in the head. He fell to the ground, dropping the briefcase. Upon impact, it sprung open, revealing shredded newspaper and nothing else.

CHAPTER
FORTY-ONE

Orangeburg, South Carolina.

The commotion outside startled Mishka so badly that she nearly pissed herself, again. The light had enveloped her in a blinding way, but she couldn't see who was outside. She guessed it had to be her father, judging by the conversation they'd had.

When the gun went off, she didn't know what had happened. She imagined one of them had backed out on their end of the deal. It didn't make much of a difference who screwed over who because she knew in the end it was her who'd lose.

As she waited for her demise, her heart hammered in her chest. She watched as a man she didn't recognize climbed into the truck and approached her. He was much too young to be her father.

"It's okay, ma'am," he spoke softly. "I work for your father. I'm here to set you free."

The chains jostled as he worked diligently to free her. When her arms dropped, the feeling of blood rushing through her veins nearly made her faint. She hadn't gotten that circulation in her arms in a long time. They'd been held above her head for so long her muscles ached.

When she fell from her bindings, the man caught her. "It's okay," he whispered as he hoisted her up into his massive arms. "We're going to get you out of here."

Together they walked to the end of the trailer where she got the first glimpse of her father. He smiled at her in an amused, simple smile. "Mishka, it's good to see you again. It's been so long."

Lester's body lay on the ground covering a pool of blood.

Tears streamed down her face as the man brought her down from the trailer and placed her into the back of the Mercedes. It didn't take long for them to disappear, leaving Lester and the truck behind.

She cried as they drove.

Turning around in his seat, her father said, "It's alright, Mishka. You're safe now. The worst is over."

These words hit her strangely because she'd never thought about her father and safety in the same sentence. She couldn't even fathom the idea that he wasn't going to kill her.

She muttered, "You're going to kill me."

His eyes grew wide. "Why would I have gone through all this work to get you if I wanted to kill you? I could have just left you with him. He'd have done it eventually."

Wiping at the snot that had run out of her nose. "You mean you're not going to kill me?"

He shook his head. "I'm going to set you free. It's the least I could do after all these years." He chuckled. "Where would you like me to take you?"

Sitting up straight, Mishka said, "All my life people told me that you wanted me dead. Now, you're here telling me that you want to set me free?"

He nodded, as if he'd seen this conversation coming. "Ah, yes.

That's how the story goes from your perspective. Not mine. I didn't want to kill you. My ex-wife wanted me to kill you. I wanted to hide you."

"You left me to die," she blurted.

"You didn't, and now I'm making up for my mistakes. You're welcome."

She couldn't bring herself to look at him, much less thank the man who'd been after her for as long as she could remember. She stared out the window, wishing the ride would be over soon. She'd instructed him to take her back to Atlanta.

Instead of driving across the country, they got a hotel room not far from the airport. Once there, she was fed, bathed, and clothed. The guard bandaged her hand with supplies from a local pharmacy. Her father not only got her a plane ticket, but a cellphone.

Standing in the doorway of that hotel, he looked her over with a fatherly, loving look she'd never seen before. It unsettled her greatly. There were far too many wrongs in their past for her to forgive him, or even trust him. She believed he knew that.

"I've done the best I can for you, Mishka. I wish there were more, but unfortunately, you're going to have to make the last leg of this journey on your own. I know what I've done will never make up for everything else. I know this, but I need you to understand that since my wife passed, I've had a great change of heart. I'm not the man I used to be."

He didn't try to hug her, and, in some ways, she was grateful for that. She watched him leave, not bothering to wave as he went.

With a shower and brand new clothes, she felt like a new woman. She couldn't wait to board the plane and return to Atlanta, where she could resume her life. She couldn't wait to meet back up with Harry and never let him out of her sight again.

As the Uber drove through the city, Mishka thought about all the things she'd missed out on. The things she'd gone through and the things yet to come. As she did, she picked at the bandage covering her hand. Many years of therapy were likely in her future as well. She'd been so deep in thought she almost missed the billboard staring back at her. A billboard of her in a black leotard, advertising an upcoming magic show. Tears of joy welled in her eyes as she stared up at it in awe.

OTHER BOOKS BY
CLARENCE CARTER

Stand Alones
No Honor Among Thieves
The Blacktop Kings
Shadows & Keyholes
The Latchkey Kids
Damn Ernie
The Rejected Ones

Anthologies:
The First Stain
Coffin Blossoms
Night Terrors Volume 22
Paramnesia
COLP: Desert/ Dessert
Home Sweet Horror
Bad Spirits

For more information check out:
www.clarencecarterauthor.com